Bridget,

With very best wishes,

Ken,

Hampton Grammar School
in wartime
1939 – 194─

G000291629

KEN RICE

PRÆSTAT OPES
SAPIENTIA

Published in the UK by
Hampton School
Hanworth Road
Hampton
Middlesex TW12 3HD

First published 2009

ISBN No. 978-0-9522113-1-0

Production:
S2DO
56 Wordsworth Road
Hampton
TW12 1ER
Designer: Jiri Musil

Front cover: Image composite by Jiri Musil based on photograph of Hampton School in summer 1945 (*Ron Keevil*)
Back cover: From Pat Gubbins' 1940 diary (*Charles Letts Ltd and Pat Gubbins*)

Message from the Chairman of Governors and the Headmaster

We are delighted that Ken Rice's 'Hampton Grammar School in wartime, 1939 - 1945', has come to fruition. We knew from his history teaching and from his recent work as joint author of 'School by the Thames' that this would be an entertaining and well researched account of what happened in and out of School during the war years. It lives up to our expectations and we commend it to the School community.

In national terms, this is a most unusual work. While books have been written about evacuated schools, we understand that this is probably the first study of a British senior school remaining at home throughout the Second World War. During the summer holidays of 1939, the school had moved lock, stock and barrel to a new site in Hampton, so the outbreak of war was hardly a propitious start. What happened over the following six years is a remarkable story of devotion, dedication and hard work on the part of the masters and mistresses, about boys who will always be boys, and not a little good fortune.

This is a thoroughly "good read", using both documentary evidence and contributions from Old Hamptonians of the period, and has been beautifully produced with the help of former Hampton School parent Jiri Musil. The School owes Ken Rice a debt of gratitude for an inspirational idea and his services freely given to produce a publication to be sold in aid of the School's bursary fund.

Hampton School 2009

Chairman of Governors

Headmaster

Foreword

No country – certainly not Nazi Germany, and probably not even the Soviet Union – was so completely mobilised for war as Great Britain during the worldwide conflicts of 1939 to 1945. This was to no mean effect. Historians have long recognised the crucial importance of the "Home Front", both for ensuring national survival during the crisis of June 1940 and in securing eventual allied victories in Europe and the Far East five years later. But even the finest of their accounts, from Angus Calder's 'People's War' to Juliet Gardiner's 'Wartime', have tended to concentrate our attention upon the most obviously transformative effects of ensuing domestic disruption: of so many displaced children during the early years to that (friendly) American invasion towards the end; alternatively, in the long-term significance of women's work in munitions factories to the short-term traumas of Bevin boys sent down the coal pits. Yet, and in this war perhaps more than any other, they also served who simply went on doing, as best they could under such extraordinary circumstances, what had previously proved difficult enough prior to the outbreak of general hostilities.

Hampton Grammar was a fine example of a non-evacuated senior school in the London area. The history of what happened there during those momentous years has never been told before. Ken Rice's stirring narrative will captivate any loyal Lion man. But his is also a serious and sombre tale that should prove of interest far beyond the Hanworth Road. For if Hampton came out of the Second World War well – and it did – such collective good fortune owed little to chance. It was far more the hard-won reward of countless individual acts of foresight, effort and self-sacrifice. The gains were real enough. Hampton boasted one of the best ATCs in the land by 1942. It also secured some of its best academic results to that date in the summer and autumn of 1945. But so too were the losses. There is something very salutary in learning that three successive School Captains – along with 119 other Old Hamptonians – failed to make it through to peace time.

Yet the real merit of Rice's account lies, I believe, in its emphasis on the massive impact of ordinary heroism. These chapters tell the story of a Headmaster who strove to maintain (and improve) standards, whatever the distractions. They also bear witness to assistant masters who fulfilled their academic duties during the day and then served as fire watchers at night; and even, amazingly, prefects who performed ever more onerous tasks while 'never abusing their authority' (p 78). True historian that he is, Rice never passes over the School's failings at this time, nor even the sad instances of those who failed to make much of their time there. For all that, the real gratitude of so many for what the School did for them shines through the reminiscences of most who were actually there. To my great surprise, I found that as I read these stories, I remembered many of these men in their later lives. I played cricket with Pat Gubbins, Vic Rice-Smith, Mick Savage, Ken Skelton and Jack Wells at the Old Hamptonians, during the 1970s. Friendly as they were to an insufficiently curious youngster, they never told me a thing about these years, or their part in them. It is thus a real, if belated, privilege to have gained such a valuable insight into their (very different) adolescent world at last.

S.J.D. Green, Fellow of All Souls College, Oxford, (OH, 1970-77)

Preface

The purpose of 'Hampton Grammar School in wartime, 1939 - 1945' is to bring out the life of the School and its pupils during the Second World War. It is not meant to be a compendium of membership, activity or achievement. As far as my sources have allowed me, I have attempted a worm's-eye as well as an over-view of life in and out of school.

The School's circumstances after the end of the summer term 1939 were extraordinary. A lock-stock-and-barrel move within the village of Hampton, from the old Upper Sunbury Road site to Hanworth Road, coincided with the imminence of war. A discussion of the move, intermingled with the consequences of the outbreak of war, what it was like for new boys to join the school in the late 1930s and early 1940s, and the topsy-turvy period of the Phoney War, provide close perspectives of the uncertainties during those years.

Subsequent events and developments, dictated by the war, through the Battle of Britain, the Blitz and the flying bombs and rockets period, are treated chronologically, with excursions into wartime areas such as Air Raid Precaution duties, school dining arrangements, and the blackout.

Three key lines of activity appear in this history: those of the masters and the mistresses, the pupils, and the Headmaster, with the Governors' support. My account turns initially to the masters and mistresses who, with the Headmaster, 'Bossy' Mason, held the School together at that time. It will become apparent why I leave an appreciation of Mason to the final pages of the book.

Writing about the 'boys' is not easy, because although – even more than sixty years on – they are willing to talk about themselves and each other on a superficial level, more rarely do they reveal their innermost feelings on personal matters. The prefects, the Headmaster's 'non-commissioned officers', performed an important function in the life of the school. Their standing in the eyes of their juniors will soon become apparent. Tales of adolescent behaviour appear in most sections of this book. The size of the fish, though, sometimes depends on the imagination and humour of the fisherman, and there are stories of alleged misconduct that I have omitted, for the sake of probity and a 'PG Certificate'. What is of interest is the cooperation between Hampton Grammar and The Lady Eleanor Holles School during the war, which I have treated through the more formal and less formal relationships between the boys and girls.

There were, of course, some boys who struggled to keep afloat at Hampton, for academic or for other reasons or both. In one instance, an Old Hamptonian has provided a fascinating insight into how things went wrong with him. As we shall see, the Headmaster and the Governors were put to the test over their treatment of the 'failures' and their ambivalent attitude towards extra-curricular activities. Mason himself provided a revealing insight into his disciplinary system in an article in The Lion less than three year into his retirement.

I have not attempted to re-construct day-to-day life, per se, in the classroom: the stuff of academic schooling then could have pertained in Hampton classrooms long before and long after the war. Certain organised extra-mural activities were either contextually significant during the war, or were the product of war itself. I have mentioned most, and concentrated on a few of the more important and interesting. Treatment of what happened 'out of school' in the lives of pupils has been limited by a shortage of evidence; in the case of the staff, other than the briefest of glimpses, I have been unable to offer any sort of assessment, such is the paucity of information. Reminiscences of how pupils' families tried to 'make do' on the Home Front could have applied to many other families in similar circumstances elsewhere. The stress and emotions in a community at war do reveal themselves at various points, even though the contributing participants to this account rarely set out to describe these.

The final sections of the book include appreciations of the roles of the Headmaster and the Governors. AS Mason bulks so large in the preceding pages that a separate section on him might seem almost superfluous; however, this history would be incomplete without it.

The survival of Hampton Grammar School was not inevitable – good fortune played its part. Yet in the summer of 1945 – as I have attempted to show in the Postscript – it was in extraordinarily good shape, thanks to those who had tried so hard to make this possible through six years of inordinate difficulty.

It is with the best and most hopeful of intentions that, in writing this History, I have threaded my way without too many mishaps, through the kind of minefield that faces all historians of contemporary events and their actors. By omission, I may have offended those who could have contributed their source material but, for what ever reason, did not. To them I apologise. During the closing stages of authorship, I discovered, on enquiring of the British Library and Imperial War Museum, that no monograph about a United Kingdom non-evacuated senior school during the Second World War, has been lodged with them. Unique or not, I hope that what ensues about Hampton Grammar School, the reader will find interesting.

Ken Rice

About the author

Ken Rice was educated at Prince Edward School, Harare, and at Rhodes and London Universities. Now retired and still living in Hampton, he taught History at Hampton School for more than thirty years. He is the author of 'Middle East since 1900' (Longman 1989), 'Garside's Wars' (Hampton School 1993), co-author of 'School by the Thames' (James and James 2005), and he contributed an article on Hitler and the Law, to 'History Review' (March 2008).

Sources

It has not been easy to assemble a portfolio of sources that facilitates a balanced approach to what is essentially a social history of the School community at that time.

The secondary sources have provided the essential chronological background. In addition to the short accounts in James, Garside, and Wild and Rice, I used Paul Barnfield's admirable research of the facts of the bombing war as these affected the Borough of Twickenham.

Problems of balance surface in the primary sources. The Hampton School Archive has at its core on the one hand, two hitherto unseen sources, namely the minutes of Governors' meetings and the 'The Russia Account', that view the School from above. Mason's 'Russia Account', a detailed description of the School as an educational establishment, was written by the Headmaster in the summer of 1945 at the request of His Majesty's Government for the information of the Russian Soviet government. It is almost entirely bland in style and content, and essentially a view 'ex cathedra'. Its most extensive section, for instance, describes academic subject syllabuses. The minutes of Governors' meetings – terse, dry and dispassionate – provide useful information concerning Mason's views on school matters and of Governors' decisions on a number of school issues. Yet the collective or individual opinions of the Governors are rarely expressed. There is no hint of discord between the executive and the board: the Headmaster and 'his' Governors seemed always to act as one.

The School magazine, The Lion, is probably the most neutral and productive source of information to hand, despite wartime and magisterial censorship. It provides a termly guide to what went on at the School and goes further than the sources already mentioned. It supplies numerous nuggets of information and opinion that an 'official' sources might ignore.

A history of this kind has to get to grips with the pupils and staff of the School. The sources of reminiscence have been invaluable, although essentially anecdotal and from former pupil eye-witnesses. More than sixty years on, grey haired gentlemen are not in the least bit reticent about their teachers, yet their memories are vivid, essentially sympathetic and appreciative. Only one longer-serving wartime member of staff has received a less than favourable press from some of his former pupils. Personal relations between boys at school were, on the surface, more formal than they are today, accentuated by the use of the surname, by boys as well as staff, as a form of address. The School's record cards omitted first names in their briefest of resumés of essential information about individual pupils. The reminiscences do provide information about life in and out of school that rings true, but in their 'anecdotage' such sources are also liable to create or perpetuate myths.

An imbalance of representative material is most obvious concerning the masters and mistresses. I have been unable to unearth any private papers of deceased former staff relating to their work at the school. Garside's memoirs are useful only for his reflections, as a Hampton resident, on the trials of the Blitz. A disappointing area of research turned out to be AS Mason's papers that were lodged some years ago with the Imperial War Museum. These were found to comprise solely of letters and cards he received from Old Boys and staff serving in the armed forces, most talking guardedly of their general experiences on active service. None of these sources refer usefully to experiences in or out of school before or during the war. Set against this, the collection highlights by implication the great respect a headmaster and many of his former students had for each other, war or no war. What some Old Hamptonians got up to during the war has already been dealt with in James' 'Hamptonians at War'. Only three memorials or interviews were produced for The Lion by staff in their retirement. I hope that this imbalance in source availability has not affected my presentation of views concerning the Headmaster and his staff and their efforts on behalf of the School and its pupils.

Acknowledgements

In writing 'Hampton Grammar School in wartime, 1939 – 1945', I am indebted to the Chairman of Governors of Hampton School, John Roberts CBE OH, and the Headmaster, Barry Martin, for their most kind Message of support; and to Dr Simon Green OH, Fellow of All Souls College, Oxford, for his generous and stimulating Foreword.

I am especially grateful to the Headmaster, Barry Martin, whose enthusiastic commitment to the project never wavered and who endured so good-humouredly many major and minor interruptions on its behalf. The School Archive has been invaluable to my researches. Dr Tim Leary, the School Archivist, has been most kind in his specific help and support. Thanks are due also to his predecessor, Marianne McCartney, the School Librarian, and School librarians, Sue Roberts and Janice Axton. The Bursar, Michael King, and the School's IT department under Ian Trevena, have provided indispensable technical assistance in my struggle towards the finishing line. A particular word of thanks goes to Maria Jafrato, secretary to the Old Hamptonians, who facilitated my vital contact with the Old Hamptonian contributors to this volume. I am grateful to Bryan Brown, the School's Development Director, Katherine Shaw and Peter Smith who have provided important help in bringing the history to the attention of the wider School community and the general public.

I am greatly indebted to Jiri Musil who has masterminded the production of a beautiful book; to the 'Honorary Editor', Fiona Martin, whose skilled and incisive overseeing of the text has saved me from so many infelicities and inaccuracies (if any remain, they are entirely my fault); and to my wife, Diana, for her perceptive advice and painstaking work on the early drafts.

A number of Old Hamptonian participants in this most dramatic five years in the history of the School came forward in response to my requests for eye-witness sources. Their oral or written testimonies, or both, have been a sine qua non of research. It would be invidious to single out any persons in particular: each and every one gave of his time and support most generously. They are Dennis Barnes, Ray Blackwood, Robin Bligh, Michael Brudenell, Ian Cameron, the late Sir Robin Catford KCVO, John Claxton, Charles Cleall, Professor David Cusworth, Alan Duddy, David Fisher, Derek Fisher, David Franklin, Charles Goodridge, Pat Gubbins, Peter Heims, Stan Holtom, Ron Keevil, George Kerpner, Mike Leahy, John Lovesey,

Clive Mabb, Dennis Marriner, Alan Meacock, the late Peter Mills, Bernard Nightingale, Vic Rice-Smith, Derek Rippengal CB, Michael Savage, Mick Sharp, Ken Skelton, Bob Smith, Dr Michael Tadman, Dr Stanley Tanner, John Warmington, and Jack Wells. Special thanks for their assistance also go to Betty Knight, sister-in-law of Jack Knight, a wartime Captain of School who died on active service; Peter Bailey of the Sunbury Local History Society; Jane Baxter at the Local Studies Collection, London Borough of Richmond upon Thames; and Phil Crookes, Cemeteries' Division of the London Borough of Richmond upon Thames.

Sincere thanks for special permission from the following to reproduce or quote from their material: Paul Barnfield; Michael Brudenell; Ian Cameron; John Claxton; David Franklin; Pat Gubbins; Hampton School Archives; Hounslow Library Local Studies unit (Middlesex Chronicle extract); Betty Knight; The Random House Group Ltd; the Local Studies Collection, London Borough of Richmond upon Thames; Richmond and Twickenham Times; TSO; Royal Veterinary College; and the BBC, whose WW2 People's War is an online archive of wartime memories contributed by members of the public and gathered by the BBC. The archive can be found at bbc.co.uk/ww2peopleswar.

Photographs
My thanks to the following for permission to use their photographs: English Heritage. NMR. Aerofilms Collection (41); David Franklin (79, 124); Getty Images (23); Imperial War Museum (22, 57, 101, 111); Ron Keevil (76, 87, 105, 123); Betty Knight (79); Lincolnshire County Archives (61); John Lovesey (131); Alan Meacock (85, 104); and John Sheaf (41, 61).

Ken Rice
Hampton upon Thames
March 2009

Contents

Prologue

War seemed on the way in 1936. In December, Donald Grant, a visiting lecturer on international relations, prophesied it in a talk at Hampton Grammar School, entitled '*The present dangerous state of Europe*'. Bernard 'Gassy' Garside, head of history at Hampton, was convinced:

'*If anyone had told me in 1919 that I should ever be in the army again, I should have thought it a very grim and ill-chosen joke ... By 1936 it had become more than a joke ...and by 1937 I had joined the Officers' Emergency Reserve.*'

The Spanish Civil War, in which Hitler, Mussolini and Stalin were cynically involved, grimly portended growing instability in Europe. In south west Middlesex, the local authority put on an Air Raid Precautions exhibition early in 1938 at York House, Twickenham. The Munich Crisis in the autumn galvanised the fitting of gas masks to more than 600 local men, women and children at the old Grammar School on the Upper Sunbury Road. Trench-digging was started on the school field in October 1938; classes in first aid, including gas lectures, resumed at the school in the new year; and all the while the builders at the new twenty-five acre Grammar School site on the Hanworth Road worked ever more energetically to finish the buildings by the end of the summer holidays of 1939 – and who could tell, before an outbreak of hostilities somewhere in Europe.[1]

Hampton Grammar School was ready for grander premises. Founded in 1556, the School had resided on two sites, once nestling behind St Mary's Church on the Thames in Hampton, and after 1880, in an imposing building with a playing field half a mile to the west on the Upper Sunbury Road, overlooking the great Metropolitan Water Board property that fronted the river. Due to local circumstances, school numbers were on the verge of collapse at the end of the 19th century but the Grammar School was rescued by the inspired headmastership of WA 'Bossy' Roberts and a Government measure in 1910 that enabled schools like Hampton to incorporate themselves in the state education system, while retaining their voluntary status, with an independent board of governors. The School went from strength to strength in spite of the Great War, and took up a new headmaster, AS Mason, on the retirement of the revered Roberts in 1924.

---

1   This, in the estimation of 'Gassy' Garside, Hampton -upon -Thames' and Hampton School's pioneering academic historian, was to be the School's fifth or possibly sixth new building since the 16th century.

The Old School

September 1939

Although the Depression had stretched the finances of the School Foundation - most of the land previously owned in Hampton by now under the control of the County Authority - it was with a bold heart in the mid-1930s, that the Governors, in partnership with the Middlesex County Council, embarked upon the Foundation's most visionary undertaking since the benefactions of Robert Hammond, Nicholas and Edmund Pigeon, Captain John Jones and Nathaniel Lacey in the sixteenth, seventeenth and early eighteenth centuries.

The Summer Holidays 1939

The summer term of 1939 ended on Thursday, 27 July. It was the end of an era at the Upper Sunbury Road site, home of the Grammar School for the past sixty years. None could foresee that the summer fête, the last great communal activity of the school year, would not be held for another seven years. Those that used the twice-daily steam-hauled scholars' train from Twickenham to Hampton – nicknamed 'The Grid' – were not to know that it would never run again.[2]

For many, the school holidays proceeded normally. Families went off to the coast. Fourteen year old Pat Gubbins travelled down with his parents and elder brother to an uncle and aunt in Callington, near Plymouth for the last two weeks of August. Robin Catford, about to enter the sixth form, was in Shoreham. His family often rented a bungalow from a friend, on the pebble ridge at Shoreham Beach where the view seawards, Catford recalls, was '... *entirely devoid for days on end of anything afloat, from coastal tramp steamer to the smallest rubber dingy.*' With the alarm bells of war ringing, on a glorious early September day, the Catford family headed back to Hampton in their car (nicknamed 'Dasher'), while the Gubbins family decided that all except young Pat would return to Hampton on Saturday, 2 September – Pat's father and brother were due to start work again on Monday in the City. Pat would stay on with the family relatives in Cornwall.

No adult, let alone parents, in that summer holiday could not to be aware of growing national tension and the government's preparations for war. Gubbins'

---

2   In retrospect the end of 'The Grid' was no bad thing. Junior HGS boys were sometimes given a hard time on the journey by their elders, being launched onto luggage racks, stuffed under seats and worse.

parents were very worried – his father had been badly wounded on that terrible first day of the Battle of the Somme, while his mother had been a nurse in France in 1916. ARP wardens had already been recruited. Housewives were being advised on official plans for food rationing. As the Borough of Twickenham had been classified as a 'neutral area', it was not envisaged that Hampton Grammar School would be evacuated. Misgivings over this 'neutral' classification, however, were expressed, due to the presence of the National Physical Laboratory in Teddington, an obvious bombers' target in a heavily residential area and scarcely a mile from a dozen schools, including Hampton Grammar. Moreover, it was months before Hampton residents received their Anderson outdoor shelters, a shortfall of more than 4000 shelters still pertaining in the Borough of Twickenham in December 1939.

On 1 September, as the Nazis marched into Poland, the British government declared the 'evacuation'. While thousands of children began pouring through south-west London by road and rail, en route to 'safe areas' west of Reading, Hampton Grammar School stayed put.

The Move

Five weeks earlier, even before the boys went off for their holidays, the school had been busying itself with the move to the spanking new school-to-be less than a mile away on the Hanworth Road. At the heart of the move was the Headmaster's secretary, Marjory Brown:

'The clouds of war were gathering and although the new building was scheduled for occupation in September 1939, many of us wondered if we would ever get there ... The great 'Pack Up' began and the move was on, war or no war. This went on steadily for weeks until at last furniture, stationery, books, sports gear, in fact everything conceivable had been moved, including that wretched Roneo machine, into the new building ... True, the new building was not completely finished and the front of the school resembled a builder's yard, but we were in, which was the main thing.'

In, but not quite. According to school records, the transportation of essential equipment and furniture was by no means complete. From 28

August, F. Bonfield's vans, which had been used for the move, stood in the grounds of the Percy Road junior school with red crosses painted on them. The incompleteness of the move meant, for instance, that there was a crucial shortage of chairs for the classrooms. In early September there was no knowing when the problem would be resolved and the Grammar scout troop's 'trek' cart, pressed into use, was scarcely adequate. In due course, though, the Bonfield vans were released and the move was properly resumed, including the dismantling and transporting of the 'Chalet' and another outdoor hut to Hanworth Road. Even though the minutes of the Hampton Grammar School Governors' meeting in December state that the move had been completed by 8 November, only 'most' of the chairs for the classrooms had been delivered.

War

On a gorgeous Sunday morning, 3 September 1939, war was declared. While none of the Old Hamptonian contributors to this account will forget the day and Chamberlain's solemn, flat-vowelled broadcast, they remember the occasion in different contexts. Eleven year old David Cusworth, as usual, sang that morning in St James Church choir, Hampton Hill. The Duddys were still holidaying with relatives in Motcombe in Dorset. Although Alan remembers his parents' worrying and listening to the speech, '... *I wasn't too concerned, being only 11.*'

As soon as Chamberlain had finished, 13 year old David Franklin's mother '... *rushed to the kitchen, picked up four gas-masks and ordered us to put them on ... Before we could object the sirens started to wail, frightening the sea-gulls in the garden. We all wandered around aimlessly with our gas masks on, sweating profusely, wondering what would happen next and then rushed to the window to look for the imminent arrival of the Stukas. After seeing nothing but seagulls settling down peacefully on the Thames, Dad quietly took off his gas mask and calmed us down as the all-clear steady note sounded. "Idiots", he grunted.*'

Still in Cornwall and having listened to the speech, Pat Gubbins' memory is, '... *that afternoon we went to the top of Kit Hill and could see the barrage balloons circling Plymouth, quite a sight.*' Less than two weeks later, Pat was back in Hampton, a return influenced by the absence of enemy action in the British Isles. Peter Mills, who had won a scholarship to Hampton in 1939, evacuated with his parents to North Devon at the end of August, even though they lived in 'neutral' Twickenham. After 10 year old Peter had spent a couple of weeks at Bideford Grammar his parents were informed by Middlesex County Council that their son's scholarship was not transferable. To return, or not to return. Influenced, perhaps, by the absence of enemy activity and a residual tug of loyalty towards Hampton Grammar School – father Mills and six of his brothers had attended the school between 1916 and 1936 – the family returned to Twickenham in time for Peter to attend Hampton on a designated date in October.

Getting into Hampton Grammar School

What were the backgrounds of Hamptonians in the late 'thirties and during the war? Mike Tadman and Derek Fisher believe the boys came from across the social spectrum, some from professional families, one the son of a chimney sweep, another from the Fortescue House orphanage. *'Not that any of this bothered us at that age – and, of course, it was one of the glories of the "eleven- plus" system.'*

To achieve entry, therefore, a boy, coming from either a junior state or independent school, would sit the entrance, or scholarship exam as it was then called, to win one of the 120 places at Hampton. Sat in the month of March, the exam had been the same for many years: three papers, in General Intelligence, English and Arithmetic. Hampton Grammar was the prime objective for most 11 year old boys and their parents living in south-west Middlesex. Michael Brudenell lived in Shepperton. He heard in May of his success in the 1937 entrance papers:

'*"PASSED" in the diary was followed by the entry "day of unbelievable joy" when I learned that I had been awarded a scholarship which paid my school fees for the rest of my years at Hampton Grammar School.'*

The threat of war did not affect the entrance procedure in 1939 and Hampton's pass list of 120 included boys young for their year. In 1940 the exigencies of an educational community affected by evacuations meant that the written entrance exam was suspended. John Warmington and others do not remember sitting an exam that year. Warmington believes that his selection must have been based on his Archdeacon Cambridge Primary School head's report.

It had always been the Headmaster's prerogative in exceptional circumstances to by-pass normal admissions procedures and admit able young applicants from unusual backgrounds. Two such newcomers in 1937 and 1939 were David Fraenkel and George Kerpner, Jewish boys whose families respectively had fled Nazi rule in Berlin and Vienna. Franklin's parents had been advised that of the non-boarding schools St Paul's and Hampton Grammar were top of London's educational tree. Both David and his elder brother were accepted by Hampton Grammar. Fraenkel (or Franklin. He changed his name by deed of poll early in the war) remembers:

'As Dad's English was pretty ropey, Mum decided to come to both interviews with the respective headmasters. St Paul's didn't fancy having a non-English speaking pupil in class but 'Bossy' Mason at Hampton was enthusiastic. Whether it was the challenge of having non English-speaking pupils or the fact that we were refugees I shall never know ...'

David Franklin today acknowledges a lifelong debt to Mason, Frank Steffens, the maths master, and WD James, the English master who went to extraordinary lengths to prepare him for the school. All three took it in turns in spending a few hours each day at Denmead, the preparatory school in Wensleydale Road, Hampton where Mr James was also the headmaster, *'... to get me interested in the English language.'*[3]

In September 1939, George Kerpner visited Hampton Grammar after term had begun for an interview with the Headmaster, James, and Steffens. This took place just nine weeks after he and his family had arrived from Austria. Mason first asked him about his previous school. Young George then read a passage from Kipling's 'Jungle Book', pronouncing tiger as *'tigger'*.[4] Kerpner recalls: *'Mr James did not seem unduly upset by this.'* When asked by Frank Steffens about simultaneous equations, he replied he had not yet got round to these. Steffens assured him that 3A had only just encountered them, so not to worry. He was offered a place. Six years later George Kerpner went up on a

---

3   To avoid confusion, David's adopted name, rather than the family name of Fraenkel, is used here. The School took a while to acknowledge his change of name.

4   Kerpner had had English lessons in Vienna from an Indian student who used 'Three Men in a Boat' as his textbook.

scholarship to Cambridge, having taken his Highers in one year, a feat unique in the School's academic history.

Grammar school entrance procedures may have gone back to normal in 1941, in spite of the Blitz, although memories vary on this. John Claxton says he entered Hampton Grammar from the Nursery Road primary school in Sunbury without taking an exam. He was second out of a class of 30 and three other boys went to Hampton with him. Clive Mabb, on the other hand, remembers taking the exam unsuccessfully a year young in 1941, attending Rectory School for a year, sitting the entrance exam again in 1942 and going into Hampton's first form with boys his own age.

Memories of entrance experiences differ even for 1943. Derek Fisher recalls that his family had come to Teddington from Southend in May 1940 which was considered to be in imminent danger following events in France.[5]

'We went to Denmead School [from the summer of 1940] *in Hampton ... I don't recall taking an entrance exam for HGS* [in 1943] *and believe I was told that I would go on my school results because exams were difficult in wartime. Interestingly though I recall that I was among 3 out of the 7 in our class that were chosen for HGS, whereas from a class of 50 or so in a Council School in Teddington I believe only 2 came to HGS.'*

Michael Savage has a different recollection. He was at Twickenham Preparatory School whose headmistress, Mrs Munn, prided herself in getting all her star pupils into Hampton Grammar, her preferred choice, or Thames Valley Grammar School. In 1943 he sat the entrance centrally at Thames Valley Grammar. Subsequently, he was summoned for interview at Hampton, which he believes was an indication that his test results were border-line. During his interview with SJ 'Sid' Barton, one of the masters, he was asked,

'"What does FAP mean?" Well, of course I didn't know what FAP meant. Barton told me that it meant First Aid Post. The initials appeared on lamp-posts around Twickenham where I lived. Then "Sid" showed me a piece of tracing paper with an outline on it. Did I recognise the outline? No, of course I didn't recognise the outline. He said turn it over. "Now do you recognise the outline". No, of course I didn't ... "That's Greenland", Barton said. Well, I didn't recognise it as Greenland. I was only 10 years old! But I must have got some of the answers right because I got my name on the list.'

5   It turned out that Teddington was to become more dangerous

The Strangest of Times: a school turned upside down

The Grammar School was due to open its doors for the new term on 12 September 1939. However, the Headmaster, his secretary Marjory Brown, and a few of the staff had gathered earlier, on Monday morning, 4 September. Marjory Brown recalls:

'...The main topic of conversation was the war, wondering who of the masters would be called to the Colours, and of course there would be hundreds of Old Boys who would be fighting for their country. It was indeed a very sad day although we all tried to make the best of it. The day of the boys' return was postponed and postponed ...'

The stark reality was that a wartime school could not be the same as a peace-time school. Furthermore, few schools in England were faced – as Hampton Grammar was – with the immediate consequences of a move lock, stock and barrel concurrent with the unique emergencies of war. The latter were already affecting the school's 25 acre site. The Governors, in the spring 1939, had approved an application from Southern Command for a searchlight site to be set up in the grounds of the new school in the event of war. 'Bossy' Mason recalls: *An experimental 'blackout' took place on 10th August. The news on 24th August [of the Nazi-Soviet Pact] was very disturbing, and the following day a Searchlight Unit arrived to settle near the new School on the new field.'* Shortly after the declaration of war an army detachment set up at least one anti-aircraft machine gun post on the field as a protection for the searchlight site. And by dint of a recent government regulation the school would be closed for at least a week after an 'emergency' had been declared, thus it couldn't have opened much before 12 September even if the school authorities had wanted to. Fortunately, there were no plans as yet to commandeer the premises for military purposes, but ditches were dug across several of the football pitches to frustrate potential enemy airborne landings. Cut several feet deep, the ditches' lattice arrangement was to enable football and cricket to be played on pitches in between.

*Lewis gun and crew
(Imperial War Museum)*

A searchlight site 1940
(Getty Images)

HAMPTON'S £100,000 GRAMMAR SCHOOL.

ANOTHER stage in the development of the old Grammar School of Hampton has been reached by the opening of the new school built on the charity land known as Rectory Farm in Hanworth-road—a magnificent pile of buildings midway between the Lady Eleanor Holles School for Girls and the senior Rectory School. The building itself is completed, and over 500 pupils are now being educated there in sections, according to the wartime scheme of the Middlesex County Council, but the total accommodation in the buildings is for 650 pupils. In its construction nearly £70,000 was spent, and, with the cost of the land and equipment, the total cost could not have been much less than £100,000.

Hampton to-day is happy in the possession of an old Grammar School foundation which, formed nearly 400 years ago with a bequest valued then at only £3 per annum, has been the basis of the finest grammar school in the county, which will cost the ratepayers so little that its effect will not be felt upon the rates.

In Memory of the Founder.

What Hampton owes to its original founder has not been forgotten. The head master, Mr. A. S. Mason, O.B.E., M.A., has seen to that, and over the portal is a memorial stone with an apt quotation from the will of Robert Hammonde dated March 7th, 1556, which states that this "Free School" is "A Howse with seates in yt for children to be towght in." A facsimile copy of a section of the will containing this quotation is in the library alongside the desk and chair of the head master of the old English school of a hundred years ago. By its side, ready to be hung, when a "Richmond and Twickenham Times" reporter was taken over the building recently by Mr. Mason, is a portrait of David Garrick, who during the time that he lived at Garrick Villa was a trustee of the old school. Another relic which many residents of Hampton will remember on the walls of the old English School for years after the Grammar School was erected in Upper Sunbury-road some 60 years ago, is the fine old clock, which kept time to the minute in the present school as the only timepiece in the building until the electric chronographs were installed last week. Given by William Jackson, one of the trustees "for the use of Hampton Free Grammar School in 1834," it had crashed from the wall time after time, smashing the woodwork to pieces, and was rescued by Mr. Sharman. The head master thinks it good enough for another hundred years. At all events, it will remain on the walls of the new school for all time linking the old with the new.

A Relic of Ancient Hampton.

Most remarkable of all is the portion of stonework of the old parish church, which was demolished following the damage done to it by lightning in 1827. It stands in a recess of the main entrance hall and is enclosed in a plate-glass case. All through the centuries the link between the church and the old foundation has been a very close one, and it is fitting that this stonework should find a place in the new school. "That is perhaps the greatest architectural treasure left of old Hampton," said Mr. Mason. Pointing to the initials "I.R." and the date 1501 cut in the stonework, Mr. Mason observed that the relic was older than the

Photo: Frank Dann

THE SCHOOL HALL.

palace at Hampton Court. It is in a wonderful state of preservation.

Mr. Mason explained its history. When the old church was demolished over a hundred years ago, Mr. F. J. Kent rescued this piece of masonry and had it carted to Castle House for inclusion in his summer house, and there it remained until it was discovered by Mr. Yates, the local historian. "It was the property of the Hampton Timber Company, and Mr. Saville, with public-spirited generosity," said Mr. Mason, "gave it so that it should be preserved for all time." The old church had been built so well that it would not yield to pickaxes, and gunpowder had to be used to take the building down, but these pieces are intact. The old church communicated in those days with the old school, "a venerable, barn-like building" on the north side of the chancel. Hampton Grammar School has a tradition, and those who have been responsible for the designing and erection of the new building have done well to incorporate in the new something of the old, for the Grammar School is one to which for years past the sons of old boys and their fathers have been educated.

Magnificent New Building.

A tour of the building showed that Hampton, and for that matter the other districts in Greater Twickenham it will serve, has got full value for the money that has been spent. There are two storeys in the main building, with a tower which forms a pleasing architectural feature from the road. On three sides of the quadrangle are the classrooms—bright, airy, and the doors and lentels are in the familiar black and yellow colours of the school. One passes from the entrance hall into the large hall, the walls of which are panelled in Australian silky oak. Old Robert Hammonde had made a condition of his bequest that "the said Vicar, &c., should cause a Free school to be kept in the said village, for evermore; to the intent that the children there shall be brought up to pray for my soul, and all Christian souls," and every morning the pupils will meet in this hall for

devotions, led in the singing of the hymn by the organ. This instrument cost £1,100, nearly one-half of the cost was met by private subscriptions on the part of those who feel that music to-day, more than ever perhaps, should form an integral part of the education given in our schools. The console is in the north corner, and the organ itself in the gallery at the farther end, the stage being at the other end. The hall will seat about 900 people.

"Keep Fit" Provisions.

No less important in modern education especially in these days when every effort is being made to ensure an A1 nation, is physical culture. Separated from the classrooms are the gymnasia, with two sets of changing rooms for both, so that while one class is being drilled the other can change without waiting. It is one of the few schools in the country to have as many facilities for non-stop gymnastic exercises. The dining room and kitchens are in this part of the building, and will form a very necessary part of the school till the Southern Railway decides to provide a service of trains, with a "halt" somewhere between the Hampton and Fulwell stations, for the benefit of the thousand odd scholars now being educated in the three educational buildings in Hanworth-road.

From the top of the tower one looks down on the spire of Hampton Hill Church, and farther away to the north, the Church of Harrow-on-the-Hill. To the west are hills beyond Windsor and to the south Epsom Downs.

In these days when the Middlesex Education Committee has had hard things said of it because of what it has not done in the provision of shelters and trenches, a look at the new Grammar School will suggest that here, at all events, the county is maintaining that high tradition of noble buildings in which Sir Benjamin Gott led it for so many years. The new Grammar School is a very valuable addition to the educational establishments of the enlarged borough of Twickenham.   R.B.

R. & T. Sept. 16.12.1939   *(Richmond and Twickenham Times,*

24

Indeed, could the autumn term begin at all before there was a sufficiency of air-raid shelters, before staffing problems had been resolved and, in the words of the will of Robert Hammond, the School's Founder in 1556, the school had enough '... seates in yt ...' for the boys to be taught?

In the event, the whole school did not actually meet together for School Assembly for the first time until early January 1940. By then the shortfall in 'seates' had been made up. Yet, if the yardstick of adequate provision for the protection of all against aerial attack had been applied, the move should not have occurred until the middle of the summer term. What Mason referred to as 'protective trenches' in front of the school were not under proper construction until November 1939. The Headmaster's secretary comments: '... the grounds in front, which should have been sweeping lawns and flower beds, now took on another aspect – deep trenches were dug, reinforced and roofed – very grim indeed.' The minutes of a Governors' meeting record that these partly subterranean concrete bunkers, built on either side of the front drive, were 'nearly' finished by February. However, they could only shelter 375 boys and staff. 'Strong places' in the school building had been identified early on as being the subterranean boiler room next to the foundations of the tower, the south corridor behind the stage and the area under the hall gallery. Initially, only the area under the gallery along with the south cloakroom adjacent to the 'physics' corridor were allocated as 'safe' places. But these took only 50 each, so for months there was a shortfall of more than 50 places. By the Blitz, though, further 'safe' areas had been designated, including under the hall stage, the other cloakroom and the south, or 'physics', corridor which meant that 850 members of the school could be accommodated in 'internal shelter areas', in addition to the 375 places in the air-raid shelters outside. How safe were the 'safe' internal shelter areas? These had been selected on the grounds that they were protected by classrooms or more strongly constructed walls and ceilings. In his report to the Governors in July 1940, Mason optimistically summed up the internal provisions as giving 'better protection than areas outside', by which he must have meant rather than being out in the open during an air-raid.

Crucially, would there be a sufficiency of teaching staff? A complement of 27 staff had been expected in the classroom for the new term in September 1939. However, GJ Atkins had left for another school over the summer holidays. Three others – WH Bennett, EAH Heard and JD Simms – had been called up in August and, like EM Harrison and AM Houghton who were called up in October, could go at any time. Seven other colleagues, Messrs James, Jago, Mulley, IRS Harrison, Manders, Malec and Steffens were placed on various armed forces officer emergency reserve lists. Garside had been called up but was medically unfit for active service due to knee trouble.

Mason had to come up with a solution. He did, and called it his 'emergency organisation'. School did not start on 12 September – boys who pitched up on the day were sent home.[6] By reorganising the school day and bringing the boys back in stages, starting with the examination forms, the boys would first be taught in shifts and on a reduced timetable. Staff shortage was thus diffused, helped by the temporary engagement of several elderly, retired teachers as a stopgap.

Even then, Mason was unclear as to how many boys there would be to teach. Five hundred and fifty had been expected on the first day of the September term, a similar number to the previous few years. By the first Governors' meeting of the term in October, Mason could report a figure of 500 boys. Twenty boys had voluntarily left the school, their fees waived by the Governors, except in the case of one whose parents had neither informed the school of their son's sudden non-return, nor paid for the damage to a master's desk caused by him earlier in the year. The next month there were 510 and by mid-December, there were 516 attending classes. Seven had joined the school from elsewhere since September. Evacuees, however, numbered 29, the date of their return uncertain.

In at Last

The staggered return to school began on Monday, 18 September, with the fifth and sixth forms, including 34 boys in their Higher Schools' Certificate year. The remainder of the school, including the new boys, returned on 9 October, on foot, by cycle or trolley-bus. All were obliged to carry gas-masks. Those like Jack Wells, a first year who lived within a mile of the school, walked to school, unless they were in the sixth form and therefore could choose to cycle. For Jack, like all the other new boys, parental accompaniment on the first day was unthinkable, war or no war. The youngest in the school, Peter Mills, lived in Twickenham. Still only 10 years old, he caught the 667 trolley bus to Hanworth Road, Hampton and then

---

6   Boy scouts and sea scouts spent time filling sandbags at their local hospital or junior school.

walked the rest of the way: *'It seemed to take ages and being nervous and apprehensive, I remember feeling tired before ever arriving.'* For the slightly older refugee new boy from Vienna – George Kerpner – the first journey to school from Twickenham and experience on arrival assumed an epic proportion.

'I hopped on my bike ... and pedalled off to Hampton to make the acquaintance of my peers and coevals at last. At first it was a lonely trek, but soon another black-blazered grey-flannelled biker appeared, then another and then little groups, some dawdling, some racing each other. They gradually joined up and when we reached the school I pushed my bike into the sheds alongside the others. As I turned around I was surrounded by some 8 or 10 boys, who stared at the bike and me. All their bikes were black, mostly muddy, some with rusty patches ... Mine, however, was cream coloured with bright chrome handlebars, shiny wheel rims and spokes and a sleek, hard racing saddle – altogether a touch exotic.

"Where did you get that from?" the nearest boy asked. "Looks funny to me," another one ventured. "It's only got one brake for the front wheel," and he lifted it off the rack to test it. "Cor, it's got a back pedal brake, never seen one, but I've heard of them. Can I try it out?" I thought I had better nod and he swung himself onto the saddle and raced off, coming back in a semi-circle at full tilt. Five yards short of the sheds he pressed hard with his foot on the pedal in the reverse direction and the bike skewed around and slithered to a stop as the back wheel locked. "Good, init – but that saddle don't half hurt your balls!" he commented.'

The new boys were awe-struck by their new school. *'Amazing'*, recalls Alan Duddy, *'I was so pleased to be there, it was quite an adventure.'* Peter Mills: *'The building itself seemed enormous with vast playing fields. It bore no comparison to my junior school with its small classrooms and playground.'* For George Kerpner, with his limited command of English, the experience of his first assembly in the impressive, Australian silky-oak panelled school hall may have been somewhat different but no less memorable than it must have been for generations of other new boys at Hampton Grammar from 1939. It mattered not that only some of the school assembled that day, that the organ was a month away from completion and that there were no hall curtains as yet. Kerpner says:

'My memory of that day still remains quite clear after 67 years. The headmaster was already standing on a raised stage behind a lectern, with all the masters standing by their chairs in a row behind him, wearing their gowns. Each class above the first year filtered into the rows allocated to them, prefects standing along the side-walls, beady eyed. The head announced the number of the hymn to be sung, the boys opened their copies of Hymns Ancient and Modern and on that first morning we all united in singing "Jerusalem".'

School assembly 1940

All united at least in person, as George remembers, *'I mimed the hymn and the prayers that followed, without a sound crossing my lips, [and] I didn't understand much of the bible reading.'* After assembly, he nearly got lost, but was rescued by a big lad whom he recognised from assembly and who was lining up with others outside a door. *'"This is Form 3A, you are one of us, aren't you," he said. I confirmed this – it made me feel much better to be part of something.'*

For the first year boys, once assembly was over and before they were allocated to their forms, esprit de corps demanded that each first year boy was selected for a House, a *'... slightly unnerving procedure'*, recalls Jack Wells. This quasi-darwinian process was the same each year. John Lovesey, who arrived in 1940, describes: *'Boys with brothers, fathers or uncles who were, or had been, at the school were asked to stand on one side. They were already allocated a house. Each house captain then chose his boys, starting with those who looked most fit and able and ending with the poor souls who wore glasses and were 4 stone nothing.'* Jack Wells was relieved: *'I wasn't quite at the end of the line when I was selected, but not quite at the top.'*

Adjustment

Those who entered the new school building that autumn ought to have been enthused – as Marjory Brown was – by what seemed to be a state-of-the-art educational facility, built to seat 650 boys.

'The building was a wonderful place, not architecturally beautiful from the outside, but it was a different story inside. A spacious entrance hall with a wide staircase leading to the first floor. A most wonderful hall, and airy classrooms with

paintwork representing the then four Houses, dark blue for Blackmore's, green for Garrick's, red for Pope's and light blue for Walpole's. Four first rate laboratories with every conceivable kind of equipment, Woodwork Room, Art Room, Library, and two Gymnasia with showers and changing rooms. A Dining Room instead of a classroom as in the old building and a most spacious and modern Kitchen, Outer and Inner Quads – and above all, to my delight, I had a real Office next to AM's [Headmaster] Study. Joy of joys!'

Understandably, there was a residual nostalgia for the old school among some boys and staff. All would have agreed with Miss Brown about the architecture, certainly nothing to write home about. 'Gassy' Garside, writing in 1957, shared her view about the considerable benefits the new school offered, even though it would take time for these to be appreciated. However, the huge grounds did not yet have the tree stock of the old site while the interior lacked the cosy intimacy of the Victorian premises on the Sunbury Road. And, he said:

There were masters who missed the glowing winter warmth of the great open fires of the Grange, two in each room; and in spring the scent of the blossom as they made their way through the gardens to their forms in the Stables or the Chalet.'

One Hamptonian not entirely comfortable in his new scholastic environment was Alan Meacock, who 'loved' the old school from the day he entered it in September 1936. While accepting the move to Hanworth Road as inevitable, he sums up in a reminiscence what for some of the more senior boys in the school may have been a move from:

'... the more picturesque but less than ideal premises on the Sunbury Road, to the bleak buildings and featureless expanse of land in the Hanworth Road ... It was unfortunate that it [the new school] was built at a particularly barren time in English architecture, and the school and its two companions [The Lady Eleanor Holles and Rectory Schools] were sterile buildings that might have been better bordering the Great West Road ... The Fives courts were never used

'An airy classroom'

29

because they were the wrong size and ... [then there was]... that extraordinary patch of brickwork called the "cloisters".[7]

It has to be said the new school's teaching facilities were not as first rate as they might have been. There was no biology laboratory. Although qualified teaching was available, no biology in the sixth form was taught until well after the war. A boy wishing to go on to medical school might be farmed out to The Lady Eleanor Holles, if there was space in their Highers' biology classes.[8] There was a photographic darkroom, but no advanced physics laboratory. If Dr Manders had not already known there was no provision for the teaching of advanced physics, he was quick to improvise one out of the darkroom. A shortfall in appropriate furniture was made good by moving benches and tables from the old school in the trek cart. These were then stained or painted by staff and boys for use in the advanced physics laboratory and elsewhere.

The Task Ahead

I t was difficult for the Headmaster and his staff to re-invent the spirit of the old school in those topsy-turvy days, especially as the education that all Hamptonians received for the next few years was piecemeal. The Headmaster reported to the Governors that the school day was organised round the teaching of boys in shifts of 105. The seven exam forms were allocated two periods a week in each subject. Thirteen other forms received half of this. Classes were also held on Wednesday afternoon and Saturday morning. Saturday afternoons were given over to games. From the end of October 1939, period lengths were cut from 40 to 35 minutes, the last beginning at 3.50 to allow boys enough time to get home before the blackout. Blackout restrictions quickly bit heavily into extra-mural activities, with after-school meetings curtailed, the call-ups and ARP duties, for instance, depriving the scout troop of its scoutmasters.

The School assembled as one for the first time on the 8 January 1940. The

---

7   Meacock's father had attended HGS on a scholarship before the Great War. Contrary to Meacock's view, the Fives Courts were used later by generations of Hamptonians playing a version of fives of their own invention
8   See below

numbers were down to 496, with 21 leavers from the sixth form into employment or apprenticeships, compared with 9 in December 1938. Twenty-two left from the fifth and sixth form at the end of the spring term, twelve of whom were from the sixth and in the opinion of The Lion would '... *no doubt soon be into the armed forces.*' Yet even after January, when in theory a full timetable could be followed, staff comings and goings led to thinner teaching and disruption. It was going to be difficult under these circumstances for the examination classes of 1940 to emulate the public examination results of 1939, which Mason reported to the Governors as being *'exceptional, indeed the best ever.'*

Nevertheless, noses were kept to the grindstone: academic standards were to be maintained. The Governors and Headmaster were prepared to take action, to the point of excluding pupils for unreformed academic scrimshanking or, in one case, for misbehaviour unspecified. Yet, in the light of the severely restricted education available in the autumn of 1939, it is to be wondered on what grounds the Governors and Headmaster cracked the whip when the parents of two boys in their Certificate year were informed at the beginning of the spring term of 1940 that unless their sons showed '... *considerable improvement in their school work the Governors will have to consider whether their places in the School are justified.*'

Order

Discipline was tight. When Mason announced enigmatically in the spring edition of The Lion that there was now a new set of 3 Rs, *'riot, roll-call and religion'*, he omitted the 7th R, the rod. It almost went without saying that there would be no 'riot' at the Grammar School whilst he was in charge and the cane was certainly not spared, as the memories of a number of Old Hamptonians will attest later. Pre-war school rules from the old school generally pertained at the new school. From the first day Headmaster and staff became even more house proud. All boys still had to change out of outdoor shoes into indoor shoes or plimsolls before emerging from the cloakrooms into the school. If a boy spilt ink on the floor he was obliged to foot the bill for the stain's removal – as John Claxton had to. Prefects as usual were empowered to punish minor misdemeanours with a detention, or 'clink' as it was called. Pupil activity in the

Rules Special to War-time Conditions.

Signals
The air-raid signals to be given—for about 20 seconds each:— on the School internal electric bells are :—
Dot, dot. dot. dot—'drop to the floor at once.'
Dot. dot—dot. dot—dot, dot—'go to shelters at once.'
Dot, dash—dot. dash—dot. dash—'all clear.'
N.B. The School large bell may not be rung and whistles may be used only in the refereeing of games on the field.

Shelter Drill
The detail of the drill may be varied according to the various circumstances. The following instructions hold always, however. Inside the building, walk quickly, in single file. Outside the building, run. Inside the shelters, pass along and fill up from the far end. Keep completely silent while the roll-call is taken by the boy responsible for the attendance book and make no unnecessary noise till given permission by the master in charge. Don't sit with backs against a wall and keep your feet off the electrical heating tubes. On returning from an out-side shelter come in by the normal entrances and pay special attention to wiping house shoes clean on the mats.

Going Home
If an 'alert' lasts beyond normal school time only those boys who have previously brought a written permission from home to travel during alerts will be allowed to leave. They will be released by forms, through the main entrance hall.

School work and other activities will be timed so that all boys can get home before blackout. Special arrangements may be made for special cases.

Use of Entrance
During 'alerts' any entrance may be used for coming or going.

A.R.P. Equipment
Pails, pumps, sandbags, rakes, shades, curtains, lights etc. must—like normal fire appliances—be treated as sacrosanct.

Military Equipment
Should soldiers or military equipment be on the premises or on the field boys must keep well away unless there is special reason for the contrary. The anti-aircraft mounds and trenches on the field are strictly out of bounds.

Gas Masks
Gas masks must be carried when coming to and from School. Boys using the Senior Cloak Room (which is also a shelter) may leave their gas masks there during the school hours; others will take them from class to class.

Miscellaneous
The Old Hamptonians' ground is out of bounds. Hitch-hiking is forbidden except in special cases. Ladies on the staff may be addressed as 'Miss X'. 'Mrs. Y' or as 'Sir'—not as 'Miss.'
Boys are advised to give their home telephone numbers to the H.M's. secretary.
Rules applicable to fire watchers will be found elsewhere.

lunch hour was carefully regulated. Boys queued for lunch – eating packed lunch or, if a boy lived locally, he could return home for lunch between 12.40 and 1.15. From 1.15, boys had to choose between being on the field, reading (not talking) in the school library, doing homework under supervision in two classrooms (between 1.30 and 2pm only) and sitting in the school hall talking or listening to the wireless.

Backs to the Wall

A n absence of celebration in what should have been this most auspicious of years had already been emphasised by the early cancellation of the official opening of the new school.[9] The pervasive uncertainty of the time was no better illustrated than at the Armistice Day service in the School hall in November 1939. Only 70 boys were present at what was traditionally one of the most poignant gatherings in the school year, this collective act of remembrance now of a lost peace as well as of supreme sacrifice. A veteran of the Great War like several of his colleagues, 'Bill' Yarrow ARCO chose Chopin's Funeral March for the service as his recital piece on the new organ.

On the same day two veterans of the Great War, the Headmaster and the editor of The Lion completed their orations of sorrow and defiance for the autumn edition of The Lion. The editorial commenced, under the subheading 'War':

"Cry Havoc, and let slip the dogs of war."

9   The new School was never 'officially' opened

We are too much aware of the calamity of the war to need much mention of it in this editorial. Faint now in the clash of strife, the Fontarabian echoes of 1914-1918, of the "war to end war" still haunt our ears, and will, we hope, awaken a determination in the hearts of men to cease this madness before it is too late.

"They that live by the sword shall perish by the sword".

"Freedom is a noble thing," wrote the poet Barbour in the 14th Century and Englishmen throughout the centuries have fought for it and died for it. Once again in these words of the King the trumpet call thrills out, "Freedom is in danger – defend it with all your might".

Mason, in his Notes from the Headmaster's Desk, adds:

'November the 11th ... but 1939, not 1918. What a tragedy has overtaken us all, Schools and individuals alike! It is impossible to put into adequate words one's feelings on contemplating the broken homes, the broken careers, the broken ideals, the broken lives of a great war such as we have embarked upon. We shall never however, I hope, see added to this list a broken national will – or a broken continuity in the centuries-old history of this School ... The war has hardly begun ... but it has already left its trace on the School, at once and yet so new.'

Expressing his relief that the school was practically completed before the outbreak, Mason pays tribute to the presence of a public spiritedness amongst senior boys, to the 27 sixth formers who had already undertaken between them over 60 spells of work on the fields and gardens, *'... with spade, fork, rake and wheelbarrow. It is good to know,'* he says, *'that there is still, as there are nearly always, many boys prepared to work for the School with no expectation of any reward beyond a sense of satisfaction.'*[10] Juniors were also co-opted into Mason's 'Public Works Department'. Jack Wells recalls picking up stones for 1d a bucket, and helping to dig one or two of the early anti-airborne landing trenches, activities rewarded with 'live house points' for the annual cock house competition.

The Spring 1940 edition of The Lion echoes the Headmaster's tribute to sixth formers. In a reference, *'Digging for Duty'*, the editor declares that even though there had been something of a decline in volunteer enthusiasm, their commitment went beyond obedience, and duty, and *'even a sense of becoming big and beefy, gave way to the sense of something accomplished, something done.'* There had always been a patriotic fervour in the scouting movement. The scout troop did its bit. While some of the older boys did ARP duties, all patrols were engaged in *'National Service'* tasks, such as collection of waste paper and metal foil, books and literature for the 'troops' and distribution of posters and pamphlets

---

10   'Digging for Duty' came to be known as Mason's 'PWD' or Public Works Department

for the Ministry of Information and the National Savings movement. Here too The Lion correspondent refers to the scouts' unstinting commitment, although he complains that the scouts' appeal for cooperation among non-scouts had met with a 'disappointing' response.

The Phoney War

Phoney war or no phoney war, there was no let up in the preparation of air-raid precautions on the school premises, as we have already seen. Provision had already been made for ground staff to sleep at the school, with reasonable funding for beds and bedding. To show that the School had not yet lost its sense of humour, the two stuffed baby crocodiles stood guard from the first day of the spring term, just inside the front door.[11] By February 1940, the Headmaster could report that full schemes for getting boys quickly to the shelters had been worked out and practised within the building, However, the Headmaster and Governors were having second thoughts about the presence of the searchlight detachment. It was not that servicemen were a nuisance to the running of the school – the toilet facilities on the north side of the Outer Quad were used by them, a satisfactory arrangement – or that the moral welfare of the pupils of Hampton Grammar or The Lady Eleanor Holles was threatened unduly by the ogling and conversations across the fence, or by the interest that some boys showed in one of the young soldiers' collection of pornography. Rather, it was that the presence of a searchlight made the school an enemy target. The County Council was to be asked to request the military authorities to move the detachment, possibly to the Old Boys' grounds fronting Dean Road which had been closed from September, 1939. There is no record of the debate preceding this resolution, but the suggested solution smacked of parochial self-preservation, given that the searchlight would now endanger Rectory School instead.[12]

---

11 They remained there for more than 50 years.
12 It took more than six months to remove the searchlight detachment and its anti-aircraft machine-gun altogether from the immediate area, an event no doubt hastened by the onset of the Blitz. However, as Mason proudly reported to the Governors in the autumn of 1940, it may have been only a coincidence that the investigating staff officer turned out to be an old university acquaintance of his and that the removal occurred within a few days of this man's visit.

There was little to cheer about going into the New Year. Mason's allusion to difficulties caused by the weather was an understatement. 'The Great Freeze Up' was the coldest since 1894, with 25 degrees of frost recorded on one night. Snow already lay on the ground when the boys returned to school. The cold spell lasted, in effect, for three months, many speaking of heavy snowfalls in January and February. The Thames froze to a depth of between four to five inches, hot water systems iced up and train journeys to London could take up to five hours. Fourth former Peter Hornsby's diary entry for 15 January records the difficulties the weather could present:

'Went by trolley [to school] and stayed to dinner, owing to terrible snowy state of roads. Left school at 3.30, to enable boys to get home before blackout. Snowed again – young [sic] blizzard at Hampton. Over a foot deep in places ... worst I've ever seen snow. Grandpa got bronchitis [maternal grandparents lived with them].'

For the young, including Hamptonians, the morale booster was that there was good skating to be had for miles around, especially on the ponds of Bushy Park. At school, there wasn't yet a fuel problem, but the athletes were displeased as their season was eaten into by a backlog of house football fixtures, the causes of which – commented The Lion – were '... *the weather and "that man"*.'

Lull before the Storm

As spring came the 'phoney' war ended. On 9 April David Franklin noted in his diary that Hitler had invaded Norway and Denmark. Unperturbed, he says, *'I went to the Dominion in Tottenham Court and saw Ninotschka and Angels with Dirty Faces, with the Movietone News and the Wurlitzer organ wedged in between, and all for 1/9 ...'* Next day members of the Hornsby family went to Chessington Zoo for afternoon tea. Peter Hornsby notes wryly: *'Saw the lions being fed – one of them uses up our weekly meat ration in one meal, I should think.'* Hamptonian diarists were jolted into awareness with the invasion of the Low Countries in May. David Franklin finds that on 10 May he noted in his diary: *'Neville Chamberlain gone and a Mr WS Churchill is now the Prime Minister.'* He cannot explain why, henceforth, he reports daily in his diary of the ominous events across the Channel. And then, towards the end of May, Franklin recalls:

'Throughout the week we had seen hundreds of little boats being towed downstream. They were like dozens of little puppies being taken for a walk in Richmond Park, and the stream of boats was endless: small private yachts, rowing boats, tiny barges ... even small Mears pleasure steamers ... On 31 May we heard that in excess of 330,000 of the British army had been evacuated from the beaches of Dunkirk.'

Others remember the loss of Whit Monday bank holiday – school instead - and, on 24 May, Pat Gubbins, who kept a diary in 1940, notes that the Germans were in Boulogne, the sound of the guns could be heard and that there was an Empire Day service at school.

'Religion', one of Bossy Mason's new 3Rs, now seemed to be assuming a greater significance for many. Gubbins and Hornsby made a special note of Sunday 26 May. Hornsby wrote: *'DAY OF NATIONAL PRAYER. Church in the morning, where I have never seen so many in a church. Absolutely packed. Went with Mother, Father, Pam, Auntie Elsie.'* Gubbins writes: *'National Day of Prayer. I went to Hampton Court*[13] *with a school friend, Geoffrey Sterling. Church full. Came back and went to St Mary's Hampton (our church).'*

Within a month France had fallen. Few could have been in any doubt that the war would soon threaten lives on mainland Britain. For the rest of term at a grammar school in outer south-west London an air of unreality seemed to pervade life at school and the lives of its pupils. Since March, there had been an unusual number of leavers (22) from the Hampton upper forms, the sixth formers no doubt soon destined for the armed forces. There were air-raid drills and air-raid warnings, but no bombs.

Looking back, more than 65 years later, Pat Gubbins remembers it as an *'amazing summer but we at school were carrying on as normal, marvellous when you think of the worries our parents and masters had.'* Normality for the adolescent Gubbins and, one suspects for numbers of other Hamptonians, meant school order cards, homework, the occasional detention *'for being in the form room'*, endless games of cricket when it wasn't raining, going to the cinema and hanging out with pals in Carlisle Park. Yet worries there certainly were, and not just to do with the war. Gubbins' father was seriously ill and in and out of hospital, to which the boy refers in his diary. Peter Hornsby's father worked in Cambridge and came home at weekends. For the Fraenkel family, one week there was the joy of David's presentation with an English [!] prize by an Air Vice Marshal at the School speech day ceremony, followed ten days later by a knock on the door and the departure of his father and brother for an internment camp. To the Fraenkels,

---

13   His Majesty's Chapel Royal

Jewish refugees from Nazi Germany, it must have seemed like something out of Alice in Wonderland.

School speech day in itself evoked a curious mixture of experience and observation. The pride of David Franklin and other prize-winners was followed by an emotional speech by the guest of honour, Air Vice Marshal Sir David Munro, who, paying tribute to the record of the Royal Air Force, referred to the greatest factors in life as *'the right temperament'* and *'guts'*, and to death as *'an easy transformation, never to be feared.'* Recording the occasion for The Lion, RC 'Dick' Rudkin, a future school captain and himself killed in an RAF flying accident five years later, says that *'... all hearts were joined in a mute, yet glorious paen of praise to those sons of England [sic] who had laid down their lives for freedom.'* Unique to the occasion, a prayer was then said asking for relief in those *'troubled times.'* However, the solemnity of the occasion was undermined by some of the assembled leaving early and the Headmaster having to remind everyone else *'in stentorian tones'* that Mr Yarrow was about to give a short recital on the new school organ. The rest of the day seemed to pass less eventfully, but the man from The Lion could not

A path through the Camp
FARNHAM, 1940

resist a priggish dig, in referring to the showrounds of the School for their parents by junior and senior boys as '... *exhibiting its modern amenities with a pride not entirely consistent with their remarks in normal times* ...'

The Battle of Britain

By the middle of July, Luftwaffe air activity had increased. The Lion stiffened the resolve of its readers: '*The battle of France is over and the battle of Britain may soon begin ... This island is, as in Wordsworth's time, the last liberty in Europe* ...' It referred obliquely to censorship, that two articles written for The Lion about the defence of a '*named*' port would have '*brought down the wrath of the censors*' and '*landed us in prison*.' Two days before the end of term, Gubbins notes that he was playing cricket when he heard explosions and machine gun fire and observed a Luftwaffe bomber overhead. It may have been the day on which Walton-on-Thames and the aircraft factories at Weybridge were bombed.

For some weeks the Headmaster and Governors had been anticipating what might be in the offing. The minutes of the Governors' meeting early in July records a plan that was drawn up to deal with the effect of night alarms on the daytime lives of staff and pupils. If air raid sirens went between 10pm and 7am assembly would be cancelled; first period would be shed if an alarm or raid lasted for more than one hour; a two hour disruption would lead to the loss of second period; while morning school would be cancelled in the event of a disruption of a maximum of four hours. Further loss of the school games' facilities was made inevitable by arranging for the Royal Engineers to cut up more of the school field '... *so it cannot be used by enemy aircraft.*'

School activities continued after the end of term, however. The Rifle Club had assumed an especially important wartime relevance and at least three shoots were held at a nearby small-bore range, with 'Harry' Crocker in charge. On 8 August, 40 senior boys and a number of staff went down to an area near Farnham for a forestry camp in hot summer conditions. Their task was to move lumber, which they did, 56½ tons of it in one week, a tiring and perilous task recognised as such by having a doctor on hand. His services, fortunately, were not required on this or another front, for, as The Lion records, more real danger lurked from the day of arrival. Slit trenches five foot deep were occupied at intervals on and after the 8th, as air raid alarms went. From this refuge, Hamptonians were afforded a *'magnificent view of airfights'* by day as the Battle of Britain got under way overhead, but less exhilarating were the bombs that *'screeched'* down on one night at least, less than a mile away, aimed probably at Aldershot's military targets. While the raids afforded the boys what, in retrospect, was *'... very good training for our present experiences'*, the camp also provided a taste of army life. Michael Brudenell, a future captain of school and holder of a scout's Cooking Badge, says he was delegated the task of preparing porridge for the camp's breakfast. In the evening he heated oatmeal in a large pan – a *'Dixie'* – and put it in a large tea chest full of hay. Overnight the hay box continued to cook the porridge *'... ready for hungry young foresters next morning.'*

For others the summer holidays, to begin with at least, provided recreational opportunities for others. Socialising on trips to Hampton Court with the opposite sex, swimming in the Thames, visits to relatives and friends, cinema going and, for Peter Hornsby, an expedition by bus, underground and tube to a gramophone record shop in Shaftesbury Avenue where second hand records were sold at half price. He bought Richard Crooks, the tenor, singing "You are My Heart's Delight" and "Two Hearts and a Waltz" for only 2/-.

The Blitz begins

Ominously, the Blitz was well under way by the beginning of the autumn term. The first bomb to fall on the Borough of Twickenham destroyed a property in Tudor Avenue, less than half a mile from the Grammar School, shortly before midnight on 24 August. Houses in nearby Broad Lane were also damaged. Entries in schoolboy diaries and memories of the remainder of 1940 are increasingly dominated by the consequences of Luftwaffe activity. Peter Hornsby's diary records:

'Sunday, 25 August, 1940

Father and I went to Kingston and saw damage done by bomb to Bentalls. Bomb dropped in the building. Lilley and Skinner's front blown out ...

Monday, 26 August
Raid at 12.30 for three-quarters of an hour. I saw a wonderful sight – the Nazi plane was dropping parachute flares. Saw 4 of them, and they lit up the whole district for about 5 or 10 minutes.'

Pat Gubbins writes in his Letts schoolboy diary :
'27 Tuesday
Dull day [reference to weather]. There was an air-raid from 9.30 yesterday until 3.45 am today. Thousands of bombers passed over. We were in our shelter for six hours.'

For John Lovesey, about to be the youngest member of Hampton Grammar School, it seemed at the time to be *'... a fantastic period in the lives of little boys. We cycled up to Box Hill to watch the dogfights. You could see a plane shot down and then after an hour could see a lorry come along with remains of a plane ... At night it was a bit more terrifying. You could hear the bombers coming over and my mother and father would get me downstairs with my brothers under the stairs because it was the only means of protection. There were no Andersons or Morrisons*[14] *at that stage. Then boys being boys, we were up as early as possible next morning to see where the latest bomb had arrived in Whitton. We would try to get under the tape which might say "unexploded bomb", get as close as possible to the crater, see what we could find and take it back to our little museum.'*

The autumn term began on 29 August, after a seven hour air-raid warning that lasted until 4am. Only about 100 boys arrived that morning and were sent home to return at 2.15 for what turned out to be only an hour's schooling. Peter Hornsby's diary reveals that the next day was as badly disrupted as any during the daylight blitz:

'Friday 30 August
Morning – school
Raid One at 11.30 for one hour. Our form and master (only 15 of us) Mr Steffens got under desks in form room at 11.25 when we heard explosions.. Then the sirens went and we went into our (cloakroom) shelter. Stayed to dinner. Heard a lot of explosions during raid.
Raid Two at 2.55 till 3.35. We went straight to our shelters this time. Went home early after raid.
Raid Three at 4.35 just as I'd got home. More explosions heard.
Raid Four at 9.15 till 3.50 – over 6½ hours. Heard planes and big explosions and gunfire.
Lovely day. 22 raids since war began.'

---

14 Types of air-raid shelters

HGS and air-raid shelters, post-war
(English Heritage)

Tudor Avenue bomb damage
(John Sheaf)

New Boys, September 1940

Prior to the beginning of term, parents of new boys had been informed that their sons' first day would be a week after the official start. If Hitler's Blitz had held few terrors to date for the young John Lovesey, these may have been as nothing compared to an encounter with the Headmaster of Hampton Grammar School on his first day:

'Bob Holmes and I cycled to Hampton from Whitton in time for Assembly in the morning. As we were about to enter the school we saw an elderly man on a very ancient bicycle, which had a wooden box on the back ... I thought he must be the caretaker and asked him what time we should attend. He told us to go home and be back in the afternoon.

Imagine our horror when we were later herded into the Hall and discovered that the man to whom we had spoken was on the stage and clad in a gown and that he was in fact the Headmaster. And he made mention that he had already met two of the new boys!'

Bossy Mason left another new boy, Mike Tadman, similarly awe-struck at Assembly on that first morning:

'He delivered an introductory talk that was typical of him – fluent, to the point and not a word wasted. The school had cost £100,000 to build. He then recalled how, in the great public schools, they proudly showed visitors the initials of future prime ministers carved on the desk-tops. "There will be NO initials carved in this school!" The portrait now hanging in the entrance hall is an excellent likeness, and captures his personality well: the piercing eyes, the prominent nose. A remarkable man.'

Imposing though Mason was, it is clear that his and the capacities of his staff and senior pupils were immediately stretched even further by the effects of the Blitz. The 'roll-call' seemed encouraging in that the numbers on the school roll at the beginning of term – 550, according to The Lion – had never been as great. But Mason reported to his Governors in October that there were *'... about [sic] 545 on the register. In certain cases it is impossible to say whether or not a boy has left. Since the start of term about a dozen have been removed by their parents to places "thought to be safer".'* No wonder Mason referred to 'roll-call' as one of his new 3Rs: there were times during the first two years of the war when he could never be sure who was, and who was no longer, a Hamptonian.

Under Fire: 'a Very Ragtime School'

Staffing difficulties continued into the new academic year. Masters had come and gone since June, six could be called up at any time, while four *'mistresses'* – including Miss Armitage, Miss GR Harrison and Miss Orton-Smith – had joined the Common Room. Most if not all the male staff were teaching by day and engaged in local defence duties by night. Mason said that his own work was *'... very reduced by frequent interruptions and my personal ARP duties elsewhere.'* Garside was a Home Guard training officer, a warden, and a fire-guard for the road and the School. Occasionally he turned up to teach in his Home Guard uniform and took turns at night along with other staff, senior boys and local residents to fire-watch from the roof of the School tower. Kitchen staff performed valiantly, providing lunches for those in the shelters during day alarms. If the sirens went during the school day, senior boys were allocated the task of plane-spotting from the top of the tower. Stan Tanner remembers his experience when, at the age of sixteen, he became a messenger for the ARP in Hampton:

'Masters were Wardens in the districts where they lived. Mr. Mason and Mr. "Jammy" W.D. James were wardens on the F4 Post in Carlisle Park Pavilion where I was assigned. My job was to accompany the Wardens to any bomb incident and to take messages to neighbouring wardens or to the Fire Service. It was the bomb on Bloxham Crescent where I saw my first dead people. We were all looking for a man. He was thought to be home in one of the bombed houses. I, being a well-behaved Hampton boy, ignored the flattened fence and tried to open the garden gate left standing on its own! It was stuck and I leaned over to see why. There was the upper half of a man's torso!'

For months, scarcely a school day would pass without major disruption. Already academic standards had suffered – there had been a 'larger than usual' number of failures in the summer General School Certificate examinations. Peter Hornsby's phrase – *'very "ragtime" school'* – not unfairly encapsulates what was on offer for a while to Hamptonians. Robin Bligh says that during September and October 1940, when daylight air raid 'alerts' were repeatedly interrupting lessons, the School worked a 36-period week timetable. Each day started where it had left off the previous afternoon, with an announcement at assembly, such as "go to period 17". Bligh remembers Frank Steffens, who took him for maths in 1B , once saying that whenever he tried to teach them algebra, the siren would sound. The Headmaster put an ironic face on the difficulties caused by air raids, referring to '... *the game of running to and from the air-raid shelters' as "a new spice to school life".*

In reality, effective teaching in the shelters was almost impossible. Until the end of day-time bombing in 1940, the junior forms went to the corridor behind the stage and underneath the gallery in the Hall, the middle school to unheated and poorly lit shelters outside, and the fifth and sixth forms to the senior cloakroom that had had a special blast wall constructed outside it. Ken Skelton remembers the semi-underground shelters:

'There were two forms per shelter that at either end had doors with glass and duckboards that floated on water covering the floor. Geography was attempting to be taught at one end and English by James at the other. On one occasion a blighter brought down a stink bomb and let it off. James was furious but we couldn't go out because the raid was still on. No-one found out who it was.'

Boys were still boys and what did the boys do if there was no school in the morning after prolonged enemy air activity at night? Not school work: instead, a game of cricket, football or tennis in the park, with an air-raid shelter to hand – as at Marble Hill or Carlisle Park - if the sirens went. Eventually the Carlisle Park boys, like Duddy, Gubbins and Wells, had their fun curtailed – not by the Luftwaffe – but by the Headmaster. Alan Duddy recalls:

'Much to the concern of Bossy Mason – because he would go up to an ARP Warden's post [near Carlisle Park] – he would see us playing ... and he wasn't best pleased about that and those arrangements stopped after a period of time.'

Twickenham boys were out of Bossy's reach. Hornsby notes in his diary:

'John and I went in the park at 10.5 am to play cricket and meet Ron there. We met Ken instead. We were just putting the stumps in when the sirens went at 10.20. John [Emerson] and I hadn't our gasmasks, Ken [Cope] padlocked his bike outside the shelters in Marble Hill, and we went in them and passed the time away by playing Nap with a pack of cards ... The All Clear went at 11.30. Ron [Whitmore] had been caught at home and came for cricket then. And we played till 12.30.'

Even though a journey to school at that time could be hazardous – boys were now encouraged to cycle rather than walk – a timely air-raid warning might encourage some, as Shakespeare had it, to creep 'like snail unwillingly to school'. John Lovesey admits:

'Our custom was to cycle as slowly as possible to school after an air-raid during the night. If an air-raid warning went you had to go into a shelter on the way and that nearly always had to be the Hope and Anchor [corner of the Chertsey and the Staines Road]. At five to nine we could go in and play cards until the all clear sounded.

Occasionally we didn't hear it and stayed on. Bossy was therefore on our tails when we arrived at school. Of course it was better to be in the Hope and Anchor shelter than in the school shelter.'

The School was only too aware of the perils of being caught in the open during an air-raid. Bombs were one thing, AA shell splinters were another. Each day numerous fragments and nose caps were picked up on the school site. Wearing the compulsory ARP steel helmet, Bernard Garside recalled patrolling the streets of Hampton during a night raid and hearing '... *funny little patterings going on all round as bits of stuff from the shells dropped on the roads, bushes, tiles etc.'*

With written parental permission, boys were allowed to cycle to and from school during an air-raid. However, the Headmaster and Governors actively sought the availability of more numerous refuges of safety at the side of roads in the Borough, proposing wayside shelters for a considerable number of children – not only from Hampton Grammar School but also from Rectory and The Lady Eleanor Holles – who were being caught in the open. In the event, brick shelters were provided by the authorities and used by Lovesey and many others. War, though, does not necessarily bring out the best in people. Jack Wells remembers:

'We were not sure how safe the shelters were, because the one up at the end of Gloucester Road [Hampton], collapsed about three weeks after it had been put up. Somebody had walked off with the cement so the bricks were only supported by sand. Really criminal ...!'

A Clear and Present Danger

The dangers during daylight raids were illustrated by an incident over Hampton on 18 September. While it may not have been accurately recorded or remembered by contemporary Hamptonians, David Franklin recalls a laconic warning from Mason at assembly next day: *"In future, will pupils observe the air-raid warnings and take cover and avoid damage to themselves and others".* Peter Hornsby's version of the incident is that at 4.42pm he was cycling home with friends along the Uxbridge Road, Hampton, when they saw a German bomber, possibly a Heinkel, flying very low, and then heard the sound of machine gun fire either from the school field's Lewis gun or from the aircraft. They heard the plane's engines cut out and saw it gliding away, losing height. David Franklin presents a different account in his autobiography. On the way to school, he and other cyclists were almost at the school gates when they heard the sound of aircraft engines and stopped to look up:

As the sound got nearer, the first came into view and a fierce argument started as to it being a Hurricane or Spitfire, as all the various identification of the silhouettes on our bedroom charts were quoted. "No, it's a Spit ... look at the wings ... no it can't be ... it's definitely a Hurricane ... the argument got quite fierce until they [sic] dived on us with all guns firing. "Told you it was a Messerschmitt!" was not greeted with much cheering ..."[15]

The Luftwaffe's 'Night Blitz' was of a different magnitude compared to its daylight offensive. For those Hampton pupils and staff living in south-west London and Surrey there were occasions during the autumn and winter of 1940 – 1941 when their community, as Hampton resident Bernard Garside put it, seemed to be *'... slowly disappearing in the darkness.'* There were very close shaves for a number. The Kerpner, Franklin and Tadman families endured near misses while, on the evening of 8 October, a high explosive bomb created mayhem in Warfield Road, Hampton, just beyond the bottom of Bernard Garside's garden. It killed four people and injured many more, destroying four shops and a dozen houses. Garside's house miraculously suffered only minor damage – smashed windows and doors – because trees and a bank at the bottom the garden deflected the blast. After weeks of the noise and effects of war close by, the incident finally unnerved Garside's wife and her mother and he evacuated them to a cousin's in Normanton, Yorkshire.

Worse was to follow for the Duddy, Gubbins and Cheeseman families. Alan Duddy recalls:

'If there was an air-raid on all night we'd go to the Anderson shelter outside that my father installed, he being in the war damage repair business ... On 9 November 1940 a bomb fell very close to the house.[16] *The properties next to us were bungalows. The bomb blasted across the roofs of the bungalows and caught our house. It took part of the roof off, put the bathroom out of commission, breaking the pan and the bath ... So we went to live with my grandparents in Teddington. On the following Friday a land mine dropped in Alpha Road in*

---

15   In a conversation with the author in April 2008, David Franklin says he remembers the sound of the bullets striking their bicycles. However, the Hanworth Road was well outside the ME 109's operational range in 1940. A more likely explanation is that the German bomber had engaged with the anti-aircraft machine gun on the School field and stray rounds hit the ground close to the boys.

16   In Falcon Road, Hampton, killing two people

Teddington,[17] *causing considerable damage to their house. So we left there and lived down with relatives in Dorset for a week until my father could get our house repaired.'*

Monday 7 October was a fine day. Pat Gubbins had had a late start to school – due to a long raid alarm the previous night – and all was well till 11.30 pm. It is not clear from his diary or memories whether the air-raid warning had gone in time for the Gubbins family to respond. However, when a bomb dropped in very close proximity to their house in Broad Lane, Hampton, Pat and his mother were asleep on the floor of the back sitting room downstairs while his ailing father was in the front bedroom upstairs. The first thing the boy knew was that he woke to '... *bricks and plaster falling on me'.* His father, unhurt, was able to get down the stairs. Pat apparently was also unhurt, but his badly bruised mother was later taken to hospital. Father and son took refuge in a house nearby and sat in chairs there for the rest of the night.

Pat Gubbins' 1940 diary: note entry 7 October
(Charles Letts Ltd and Pat Gubbins)

17   Five people were killed

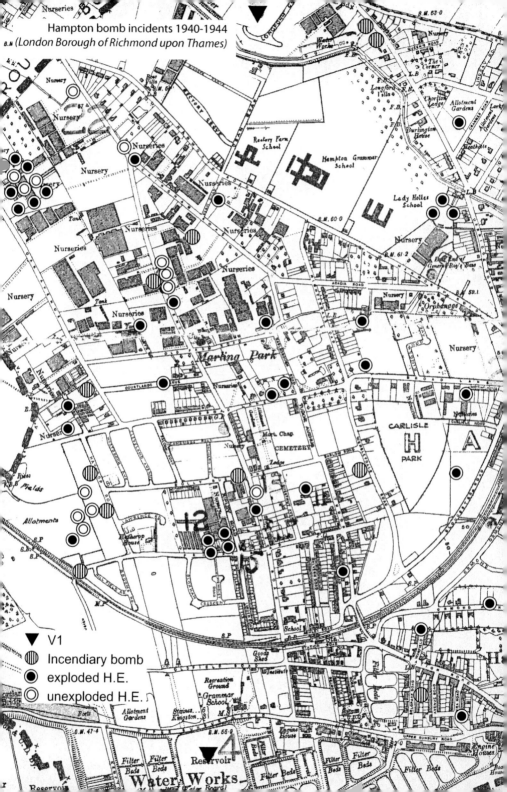

Hampton bomb incidents 1940-1944
(London Borough of Richmond upon Thames)

▼ V1
⬙ Incendiary bomb
◉ exploded H.E.
◎ unexploded H.E.

Next day, without being asked, their friends the Sterlings collected Pat and his father, taking them to stay at their house in nearby Wensleydale Road. *'They were marvellous to us,'* recalls Pat Gubbins. Later, he first went to the hospital to see his mother, still in shock, and then returned to the house to try to salvage some belongings. By the end of the following day, while recoverable light furniture was being put in a shed in their garden and heavy furniture taken to a lock-up garage at Kingsbury's in Station Road, Government civil defence workers had commenced the task of demolishing the Gubbins' semi-detached house and the one next door. Pat was already back at school by 10 October when his mother was discharged from hospital and had come to stay at the Sterlings. Critical decisions were taken within days. The family would go to relatives in Cornwall until rented accommodation could be arranged in Hampton. And Pat would have to leave Hampton Grammar School. On the 17th Mr Mason visited Mrs Gubbins. While agreeing to Pat's departure, the Headmaster said he could return if the family's circumstances changed. Without a roof over their heads, Pat's father so ill and his elder brother Jack in the Forces, this was unlikely. Pat would have to go out to work. For a promising young sportsman, academically willing, and who clearly adored his school, one short sentence in Pat's diary entry for 17 October summed up his emotions:

'I feel very miserable at leaving Hampton.'[18]

Three weeks later, tragedy struck the Cheeseman family who lived at the 'White House', near The Avenue, less than half a mile from the School. While the Cheeseman's daughter Stella was miraculously spared, a high explosive bomb destroyed the house, killing her mother, father, and Bert junior, just turned fourteen and member of Form 3a at Hampton. Ken Skelton was a good friend of the son:

'Bert Cheeseman was in our form. A delightful bloke. I can still recall his features, dark hair, very supple and a fine gymnast. He could do flick flacks and things that none of us could do. Unfortunately, it was one of the Headmaster's duties at morning assembly to record the names of senior boys who had gone in to the forces and lost their lives. To be told at assembly the morning after that he had been killed along with other members of his family I still recall with some sadness.'

A few days later, the family's funeral was held at All Saints' Church, near the blackened remains of what had been their house. Due to air-raid alerts, the

---

18   Pat Gubbins started work as a junior clerk with the National Westminster Bank in Richmond early in January, 1941. His father died the following month

Grammar School boys, other than the Captain of School, Jack Knight, were not permitted to attend. Bernard Garside remembers:

'As the three hearses stood abreast in the road with the three coffins, the raid siren went and in a few minutes a German plane droned over. There we stood, a mourning group by the church and hearses, the ruin in the background and the plane droning overhead, no-one knowing at what moment even the three corpses would be blown sky-high.'

The Cheesemans' grave lies just inside the north gate of Hampton Cemetery. Other than a boy who was injured by a shell splinter during another raid, Bert Cheeseman was the only serious casualty amongst boys and staff during the Blitz. The School itself suffered only minor damage: one pane of glass, broken by a metal fragment.[19]

Cheeseman grave Hampton Cemetery

---

19   Notwithstanding the impact of Bert Cheeseman's tragic death in a Hampton Grammar School context it was of comparatively less significance than the incident at Catford Central School for Girls on 21 January 1942 when a Luftwaffe bomb killed 44 pupils and teachers.

The School Dinner Heroes

Returning to 1940, among the school's heroes during that difficult autumn term were the 'Canteen' staff. At the beginning of the year a new dinner scheme had been launched independently by the School under Mr Jago. At 10d a meal, the worthiness of the school dinner arrangement appealed to mothers who, due to rationing and other wartime circumstances, faced increasing difficulty in feeding a growing family at midday. Half of those using the new dining room were 'cold diners' who brought a packed lunch from home, so two sittings were organised in a dining hall that sat 160. The daylight Blitz, however, witnessed extraordinary efforts by the Canteen staff to lay on dinners. When the sirens went, remembers Marjory Brown:

'Mrs Cook, or Mrs Hewitt, plus her Canteen Ladies, always dashed over to the Entrance Hall where they waited[20]*... Mrs Hewitt usually arrived with wooden spoon, ladle or some other implement, probably whatever she was using when the siren sounded. Once she arrived with a carving knife! Despite all, Mrs Hewitt always produced a good substantial meal.'*

By October, 110 paid dinners were served a day and for a whole fortnight at one stage all school dinners were served in the shelters. This must have bolstered morale significantly. The Canteen Committee's report to the Governors heaped well-deserved praise on the staff and the master in charge, Mr Jago. By early 1942 the Canteen had become part of the County School Meals Service. New refrigeration equipment was installed and the cost of a school dinner, that had been reduced from 10d to 9d in December 1940, was now reduced from 9d to 6d a meal.

Although the numbers of school meals served by early 1943 had risen to 400 a day, a question mark has been raised over the quality of food on offer. There was no truth in a contemporary rumour that school meals were 'uneatable', or in a Hamptonian quip that *'school meals eat dirt cheap.'* Rather, the consensus of retrospective Hamptonian views on the school dinner is represented by Stan Tanner, later an eminent veterinary scientist: *'While entirely adequate for growing boys, as dictated by the government dieticians, [it] was singularly lacking in its appeal to the taste-buds.'*

---

20   Not the safest place, given the hundreds of tons of School Tower masonry that lurked above them

'The Canteen'

The ingredients were undoubtedly enhanced by the inclusion of vegetables grown on site in the school's wartime allotments. The meat, though, usually consisted of spam or corned beef or 'bangers' – inevitably with 'mash'. Occasionally, there was roast beef and potato. Robin Bligh can remember being introduced to pease pudding, which he had never seen at home. He says that the caterers provided tinned fruit as often as possible, but semolina or rice appeared regularly. Derek Fisher recalls a joke about the suet pudding that was served:

'Mr Jago, the fiery French master, would come to see that the boys were happy with the food (a bit like Oliver Twist!). He was said to have picked up a portion of suet pudding to demonstrate it was wholesome but dropped it on the table and being so rubber-like it bounced!'

Jago, who, with his wife, oversaw the dinner system till the end of the war, was a controversial member of staff and we will come across him again. However, on his retirement many years later, he related an anecdote about a Blitz school dinner incident in the shelters that may reveal as much about his acidic sense of humour as about the unidentified miscreant:

'A table senior pinched a whole plateful of eight rations of meat right under my eyes, the only time anyone attempted this feat. He later got a good Honours degree at Cambridge.'

In due course some boys stopped taking school dinners, instead cycling down to the local Civic, or 'British', restaurant in Hampton village. These were Government sponsored restaurants staffed by lady volunteers. The quality, if not the price of a meal, posed real competition to what was on offer at school. In 1942, an 11d lunch at a British Restaurant in London would consist of roast beef, two vegetables, treacle pudding, bread and butter and coffee.

Fire-watching

From September 1939, fire-watching was an ARP duty that a senior boy could undertake, with the permission of his parents. By January 1941, what seemed to have been organised on an ad hoc basis was now properly constituted, its members fed and paid. A squad of between four and six watchers, comprised of a mixture of staff, Old Hamptonians, local residents and senior pupils were paid 1/6d a night each and received a free meal from the Canteen while on duty. Not until early in 1945 was the service scaled down and finally abolished.

George Kerpner recalls his work as a watcher:

'You received some rudimentary training with a bucket, sand and a long handled hoe and thus qualified spent the night at school, resting on a camp bed in a small room that had been a broom cabinet. If there was an air-raid, you were supposed to keep awake and put out any incendiary bombs that might come your way. For your trouble you were supplied with a bottle of drink to last you the whole night and a bacon and egg breakfast, which was a rare treat in those days of food rationing.'

Ken Skelton was a watcher in 1942 when air-raids were rare and there was increasing scope for schoolboy devilment. *'We were shockers!'* he admits and remembers apple scrumping as one possibility:

'Apples were ripening in the late summer and there were beauties in the orchard beyond LEH. I was on duty just before dawn. I got a satchel and put on ... plimsolls because I might have to run if a copper was out on patrol. I raided the orchard and shared the apples amongst the others.'

In a night tour of duty, watchers had access to the whole school, so raiding the larder was another possibility:

'The fridges were open and there was cheese and all sorts of things which were rationed. It was like gold to us. We were nicking this ... stuff until they realised and put padlocked chains on the door.'

And then, says Skelton, there was Mick Sharp, the Hamptonian equivalent of 'Blondin':

'A lad on duty with me was quite reckless. He would walk round the parapet of the tower, only 9" wide. He was quite nerveless and was said to have walked along the parapets of the Richmond bridges as well. On a tour of duty on one occasion, we found in the changing room a jockstrap belonging to a very well known athlete. [My colleague] went up on the tower, climbed the twelve foot mast and put this piece of sports wear over

the top of the mast. The caretaker ['Rocky' Foreman] saw it next morning and had to go up and get it off. At assembly the Head was furious but never found out who it was.'

The Blitz and its trying circumstances continued until the end of the winter of 1940-1941, each experience etched in the memory of the young. Whether it was the shocking view from Richmond Hill of the City on fire in December, or the dangers that fathers faced as they commuted from central London during air-raids, or the time-wasting ration queues endured by harassed mothers, or the nightly procession to the shelter, perhaps the greatest was the fear of not knowing whether, as Michael Brudenell put it many years later, '... a bomb had got your name on it ...'

Adventure in the Blackout

Not least, the blackout posed its own dangers and well after the Blitz was over. Early in 1944, a school outing to an evening performance of 'The Merchant of Venice' in the West End, starring Donald Wolfit, nearly ended in disaster for a fifth former, Peter Hodges. On the return journey from Waterloo to Hampton, Hodges, who lived in Whitton and was not fully acquainted with the train's route, decided to alight when the train came to a halt at what he thought must be Fulwell Station. He was wrong: the train had stopped at the signal before Fulwell.

'I ...opened the door – and stepped into space ... It's a surprisingly long drop from a carriage door to track level and I'd got myself cut up a bit on the ballast chippings. Roars of laughter from the compartment followed my exit, adjacent blinds went up – in defiance of blackout regulations – and "Hodges has fallen out of the train" spread like wildfire ...'

As an adult passenger prepared to lean out of the open door to help him, the dim compartment light fortuitously illuminated a large porcelain insulator by the track and Peter Hodges realised he had been about to put his foot on the live third rail. However, before he could clamber aboard, the signal turned green and the train left the boy standing in pitch dark, between the live rail and an embankment. After a hair-raising scramble, via a bomb site, to safety in Clonmel Road, he walked home to Whitton. At school next day the only sympathy he got from his fellows was, '... "Hodges fell out of the train, ho ho".'

Mad Hatter's Tea Party

There was no balance in Hitler's intentions for Europe, least of all concerning refugees like the Fraenkels and the Kerpners. However, if the Blitz wasn't enough to contend with, the Fraenkel family had a further run-in with the Home Office over David's alien status. Friends had previously fought successfully to have his father released from internment. In December 1940, for David, about to turn 16, having to apply for a permit to ride a bicycle and then appear before an aliens tribunal must have made him wonder whether he was now at The Mad Hatter's Tea Party. The Headmaster of Hampton Grammar School, though, was having none of it. Informed by letter of the Home Office's intentions early in December, Mason composed a pointed reply which he showed to David before sending it, much to the boy's delight. Part of it reads:

'... I cannot imagine that any harm to this country would be caused by Fraenkel having a cycle while at school. The journey from his home to this School is very awkward for all but motorists and cyclists. Some 400 of our boys cycle to this School for similar reasons.

As regards the question of internment I very much hope that that will not be necessary. Fraenkel's behaviour and industry while here have been excellent and I have never had any reason to suppose that he or his family were anything but loyal to this Country. The boy is within 18 months of taking the General School Examination and I hope he will be allowed to complete his education by staying here and working for it

(signed) AS Mason, Headmaster.'

In the event, as David Franklin says, he was allowed to keep riding his bicycle, he was not interned and he passed his GSC 'with flying colours.'

D-Day

Few Hamptonians could have had doubted by the spring of 1944 that something 'big' was about to occur in the European War. Danger from the air had never disappeared completely – a sneak Luftwaffe raid had in February distributed 28 bombs on Hampton Hill and Hampton, miraculously with no loss of life and little damage to property. However, evidence of an extraordinary and expanding military preparation in the locality was not easy to conceal, particularly the proliferation of United States servicemen – the ubiquitous GIs – based in Bushy Park. Leaving aside the role of the School's ATC unit, some senior Hamptonians were engaged in war-work that, with the benefit of hindsight, was directly connected with the expansion of logistic preparations for D-Day and its consequences. Although not documented in school records, but according to Clive Mabb, the School, and in particular its laboratories, was used as a centre for the packing of various types of spare parts for transportation to the war zones in the spring and summer of 1944. Mabb recalls:

'The first period of this work was during the Easter break ... The [school] laboratories were used as the workrooms. The goods were transported by lorries from Feltham Royal Army Ordnance Corps depot to the entrance nearest the labs. Some of the items were covered in anti-rust material which made the job somewhat messy. Hands had to be covered with a special cream to prevent dermatitis. The parts were then wrapped in brown waterproof paper and packed into stouter boxes.'

Dennis Barnes' discovery at Ham early in 1944 had an historic significance impossible to fathom at the time:

'... Friends and I had discovered large hollow concrete things floating in disused gravel pits at Ham, across the river from Twickenham. It was great fun to push these off from one bank and sail to the far bank. It was much later that we understood that these were sections of the Mulberry harbours.'

One unique effect of the war was the considerable presence of American servicemen in England after 1941, not least in their huge encampments in Bushy Park. As we shall see shortly, a couple of Hamptonians would have good cause to be grateful for the intervention of one US army unit during a flying bomb incident near Bushy Park. Other contacts were less dramatic. Major Woolley, US Army, and from California, visited the School in October 1943 to talk about America. US army officers were billeted near Bushy Park with local residents like the Fishers:

'At the time of D-day the officer who lodged with us had been a newspaper editor in peace time. He produced the Invasion Communiqué published in the national newspapers each day after D-day. I have a couple of newspapers with this communiqué.'

Dennis Barnes recalls his conversation with an American officer whilst waiting for a bus in Twickenham:

'We spoke and I told him of my plans. He explained that what I should be looking at was a career in cartography. This being what he was doing with the American forces. He offered to send me a book on cartography, which he did. I never did get into cartography, but to this day do collect and study maps from wherever I travel.'

Flying Bombs and the V2

News of D-Day thrilled everyone the length and breadth of the kingdom. Exactly one week later, however, four explosions occurred in south-east England, excited eye-witnesses believing that enemy aircraft had been shot down. It took the Government three days to announce what they had secretly anticipated for more than a year: German pilotless aircraft – 'flying bombs' – were being launched across the Channel. The Home Secretary, Herbert Morrison, warned:

'When the engine of the pilotless aircraft stops and the light at the end of the machine is seen to go out it may mean that an explosion will soon follow, perhaps in five to fifteen seconds.'

Soon there was to be no respite from these 'Vernichtung' [annihilation] weapons. They could arrive, at any time, in all weathers. For many months, as the historian Paul Barnfield puts it, '... *life was one long alert, day and night.'*

The Headmaster of Hampton Grammar School, in a report to the

Flying bomb
(Imperial War Museum)

57

Governors, revealed the impact the new menace was having on the School. He said that since June it had been impossible for the School to function normally. About 35 boys had been evacuated. The alerts were *frequent and long and coincided with University and School exams*. While the University exam candidates worked through the alerts, the school exams had been cancelled. The exams, the Headmaster says, could not have been taken under worse conditions. He reported that two flying bombs had fallen close to School property on 19 June. The one that exploded 300 yards to the north of the School property on Hanworth Road had broken two panes of glass and the fastening on one door in the main school. The other that fell into the Metropolitan Water Board reservoir blew out most of the glass in the old school across the Upper Sunbury Road.

The journey to and from school during the flying bomb Blitz could be more traumatic than in 1940 because there was so little time to take shelter once the 'doodle-bug', later to become known as the 'V1', had announced its arrival. David Fisher recalls:

'The usual route to HGS for me and some of my friends was to cycle through Bushy Park to Hampton Hill and up the Uxbridge Road to school. In 1944, Bushy Park was a huge, mainly US military base. One sunny morning in June we were cycling through the park, past lines of American tents. Nearby was a sandbagged gun emplacement with an anti aircraft gun inside. As we neared it, a soldier rushed out and wound a warning siren denoting imminent danger. A few seconds later we saw and heard a V1 coming straight towards us. The gun crew started elevating the gun to fire at the V1. Just then an officer rushed out of the tent and shouted, "Don't fire at the goddamned thing – let it go over and hit some other poor sons of bitches – get in the ditch and take those boys with you." As we dived into the ditch, the V1's engine cut out, meaning it would soon dive into the ground and explode. We watched it tip over and swoop down above us. It landed just outside the park with a huge bang and a cloud of smoke. We thanked the US officer for getting us safety into the ditch and cycled onto school shaken but unhurt. I have since thought that had they hit the V1 and it had come down on us we wouldn't have got to school that day, nor for the rest of our school careers...'

His brother, Derek, says that his recollection of that term was of not going to school every day because of these conditions. Vic Rice-Smith, then in his first year at the school, remembers visits to the school shelters during flying bomb raids, where it was impossible for proper lessons to take place, especially written work:

'Everyone talked until the drone was heard (vroom, vroom, vroom) and we became tense and quiet. When the engine stopped you held your breath waiting for the bang.. When that came you were relieved and you knew you had been scared. But then you worried about your home as most boys lived within 3-4 miles of the school.'

Stan Holtom and a friend were but two who lived not far away:

'One late afternoon as the sirens wailed, we were confined to school awaiting the all clear. I was standing with an HGS mate from Teddington with whom I had been in elementary school. As we looked skyward a V1 appeared over the school; the motors cut and the gliding commenced. As it disappeared from view, we estimated that it landed somewhere in the Teddington area. When the all clear sounded we hurriedly made our way home. As we approached the impact area we noticed increased police, fire and ambulance activity. My school mate made his way to his house only to realize that there was extensive damage. The V1 had indeed detonated in Teddington. His house was severely damaged and his mother was nowhere to be found. Death became a reality and understandably the fascination of tracking gliding V1s disappeared in this moment of despair.'

John Claxton, who lived in Sunbury, had a narrow squeak:

'One Sunday we had a lot of people at the house and we went on an expedition up the river. At the end was a weir called Tumbling Bay and it was an exciting expedition because you had to get out and push the boat over shallows. After we had started back, the air-raid siren went, which in those days meant a flying bomb was headed our way. As we arrived back at our house we heard the bomb coming (I shall never forget that noise) and heard the engine cut out. That usually meant an immediate vertical drop and so safety for us as we could tell it was still some distance away. I rushed to the top of the bank to look for the explosion and I saw the flying bomb apparently coming straight towards us - it was of the rarer glider type. I shouted a warning, then realised it was not heading quite our way. Well, it hit that weir at Tumbling Bay where we had been thirty minutes earlier. Two people were killed and the weir flattened, causing the river to flood ... I think it was that event as much as anything that caused my parents to arrange for my sister and I to be evacuated to Blackpool to my aunt and uncle, where we stayed from August 1944 till March 1945.'

The fate of Hampton master, 'Bill' Yarrow's house in Sunbury, while the entire family was away on the School summer camp, will be recounted later. John Lovesey, however, had the closest call of all. He would never forget 1944. For much of the spring and the summer he had been seriously ill with pleurisy. He had been allowed back to school during the summer term to prepare for his GSC french oral and the school internal exams, but was not allowed to take part in Wednesday afternoon games. One games afternoon, he took up a dare:

'I climbed up on the gym roof and eventually managed to ring the school bell, which had been covered since 1939. It was only to be rung in the event of a German invasion, but that seemed hardly likely as we seemed about to invade Europe.'

The Headmaster was not best pleased and must have thought that if the lad was fit enough for such strenuous antics, he was fit enough to take the consequences. He met young Lovesey as he made his final descent and marched him off to his study to give him six of the best. During the summer holidays John Lovesey suffered a relapse of his pleurisy and was away from school at the beginning of term. And then, on the afternoon of 29 August the Lovesey family, who lived in Whitton, miraculously survived a terrifying tragedy:

'My father was away in the army. My younger brother, Peter, was at Bishop Perrin junior school, my mother was out and I was at home with my 18 month old brother, Andrew. I heard the doodle-bug and then its engine cut out. We knew that if you could get to a shelter within thirty seconds your life might be saved. I took hold of Andrew and we got into our indoor Morrison shelter just before the doodle-bug struck. The house was completely demolished. The house next door had only one wall standing. The neighbours opposite and next to us were all killed. My father immediately came home to a terrible scene. All the bodies had been put under tarpaulins in what remained of our front garden and he did not know whether we were alive. Eventually he found us with friends in Montrose Avenue. Nothing was left of our possessions, save my slightly damaged autograph book. Next day we left for Cornwall to stay with my grandparents near Boscastle. It was a harrowing experience!'

Just as the V1 menace came to an end, with the Allied occupation of the launch sites in the Pas-de-Calais area, Hitler launched his second and potentially more devastating weapon, the V2 rocket. Against these there was no warning and no defence. Fortunately,

CHILDREN SAFE IN "MORRISON"

When House was Wrecked by Flying Bomb

Mrs. Lovesey, a resident of a borough in Southern England, can testify to the strength of Morrison shelters. When she went shopping on Tuesday she left her two children in the Morrison for safety; she had not long been out when a flying bomb landed in an adjoining garden. On reaching home Mrs. Lovesey found that her children were safe, although the house was a heap of wreckage. Her husband, a lance-corporal in the R.A.O.C., who was injured in a flying bomb incident some weeks ago, was sent home on compassionate leave.

The bomb fell in the early afternoon and caused casualties—some fatal. A number of houses were destroyed and others damaged. And there was considerable blast effect on surrounding property. Several cars in garages of affected houses were destroyed or damaged.

People who lost their lives were Mr. and Mrs. Vicery, Mrs. Vane, Mr. Ryder and Mrs. Alden. Of the injured, only four were detained in hospital. They included Ronald Mabberley and Ronald Milling, both aged 16.

A doctor whose house is near to the scene of the incident earned praise from many people for the fine work he did. Wardens who are relieving Civil Defence workers in the district took part in the rescue operations. U.S. troops and British naval ratings helped in rescue and repair work, and the Home Guard patrolled the area during the hours of darkness.

Members of Rescue Services were actually on their way to the spot before the message had come through from headquarters, and they did excellent work in extricating people who were buried, the last being dug out less than three hours after the bomb had fallen. The W.V.S. set up an Incident Inquiry Point and a mobile kitchen, and a few people were taken to a rest centre.

On the following day a woman whose house had been damaged considerably by blast hung out a line of washing to dry in the midst of the debris.

When a flying bomb dropped near the border of a municipal area in Southern England on Tuesday afternoon, causing casualties and damage, the effect of the blast extended to houses some distance away.

29 August 1944
Chronicle Newspapers

60

Morrison shelter
(Lincolnshire County Archives)

the School and its pupil catchment area were very little affected by the V2s. The closest rocket strike to the School was on the Metropolitan Water Board property to the north east of Kempton Park, less than a mile from the School, at just after four in the morning of 15 September, 1944. The first thing that Alan Duddy and his family heard, in Hatherop Road, half a mile away, was an enormous roar followed almost simultaneously by a heavy explosion. Not until March 1945, once the launch sites in the Low Countries had been captured, could people in south east England press on with the total dismantling of air-raid precautions such as indoor shelters.

Anderson shelter in Hampton
(John Sheaf)

The Teaching Staff

I t is time to look at the engine room of the Headmaster's command: his teaching staff and senior pupils. Their importance is already under-scored by what we have seen of them during the earlier years of the war.

There is a consensus among the great majority of those who contributed to this author's researches that, given such trying circumstances, the School was most conscientiously served by its masters and mistresses during the war. Cambridge graduate George Kerpner pays tribute to '... *all those fine teachers who had such infinite patience with us, ever intent on producing silk purses from sows' ears.*' And we have already learned of some of the schoolmasterly virtues of the Headmaster and several of his senior staff, in the context of the extraordinary circumstances affecting a school only just transplanted from its previous geographical environment.

In serving its pupils, the staff-room, as we have already seen, was under extreme pressure. At several Governors' Meetings, the Headmaster placed on record the strain caused by staff shortage. Not until the summer of 1943 could he report that he had a full complement of teachers. Miss Brown was absent for much of one term due to stress while Frank Steffens became ill in the autumn of 1943 with a nervous condition that affected his heart. Mason himself came close to a full-stop. He confessed to the assembled at Prize Giving in the summer of 1942 that he had not prepared a proper speech as he had been working up till half an hour before the event. He failed to deliver his customary

SCHOOL LIST, 1940-41.

Governors:

Chairman:
ALD. A. G. GREIG, C.C.
Vice-Chairman: A. T. SHEPHERD, ESQ. (O.H.).
CR. C. W. BECKETT.   DR. R. L. LANGDON-DOWN,
ALD. D. F. CHALMERS.   M.A., M.B., B.Ch.
THE REV. E. E. CHARLES,   ALD. E. H. NEWMAN.
  M.A.   ALD. W. T. E. OLLIS, C.C.
THE REV. PREB. W. P.   ALD. F. W. PAINES, (O.H.),
  COLE-SHEANE, M.A.   C.C.
CR. W. A. COOKE.   CTY. CR. E. ROWLAND.
H. T. CREASY, ESQ., C.B.E. D. M. SUTHERLAND, ESQ.
THE REV. F. P. P. HARVEY, DR. J. W. T. WALSH,
  A.K.C.   M.A., M.I.E.E. (O.H.),
W. O. HIEHLE, ESQ. (O.H.).

Clerk to the Governors:
H. M. WALTON, 10, Gt. George Street, Westminster.

Head Master:
A. S. MASON, O.B.E., M.A., B.Sc.

Assistant Masters:
  H. R. DAWE, B.A., *Second Master.*
R. B. Ackroyd.   *I. R. S. Harrison, M.C.,
J. T. Hartwell, M.C.   M.A.
*E. M. Harrison, B.A   S. J. Barton, B.Sc.
S J. House, B.Sc.   C. R. S. Manders, Ph.D.,
G. Hayler.   M.A. (Ed.), B.Sc., Dipl.
W. D. James, B.A.   d'Et. Sup., A. Inst. P.
H. W. T. Jago, B.A.   C. F. Jeffrey, B.A.
H. S. Moodey, M.A.   H. Crocker, M.Sc.
*B. Garside, M.A., B.Sc. F. E. Steffens, B.Sc.
  (Econ.), F.R.Hist.S.   *W. H. Bennett, M.A.
W. P. Yarrow, M.A.,   J. D. Simms.
  A.R.C.O.   *E. A. H. Heard, M.A.
*C. Mulley, M.A.   *L. Malec.
C. C. Titterton.   F. W. Kimber, B.A.

2

*L. Moorhouse, M.A.   Miss A. S. Armitage, B.A.
R. M. Bentham, M.A.   Miss M. L. Knight, B.A.
*F. W. Land, M.Sc., Ph.D. Miss A. M. Baker, B.A.,
†A. E. Robertson.   Ph.D.
†H. Parnell.   Miss P. M. Nye, B.Sc.
†*Miss L. Orton-Smith, B.A.   (part-time).
†Miss G. R. Harrison, B.Sc. †Mrs. McDermott, B.A.
      * *Serving with H.M. Forces.*
          † *Seconded to H.G.S.*
H.M's Secretary ...   Miss M. B. Brown.
Caretaker—C. F. Foreman.   *Asst.*—W. J. Cottrell.
Groundsman—W. Verth.   *Lab. Asst.*—R. J. Cox.
Canteen Supt.—Miss A. Hutton. *Asst.*—Miss D.A.Smith.

report to the Governors' Meeting at the end of 1942 and again in the summer of 1945. It is known that the Governors had privately voiced their concern about the effect the long hours he worked might have on his health. We shall consider AS Mason's extraordinary contribution to the wartime School later in this book.

The Old Guard: two Senior Masters

In the context of discipline, it was the Headmaster and a core of teachers who held the school together, those to whom Mike Tadman refers as 'Bossy's old guard'. Tadman, who joined the school in 1940, says: *'Bossy's old guard never raised their voices. They didn't need to; there was something charismatic about their presence.'*

Hampton Grammar was ably served by two Senior Masters during the war. HR 'Punch' Dawe had been Senior Master since 1932. The author of the School Song, an excellent linguist and teacher who fought in the First World War, 'Punch' had joined Hampton in 1905. The man with the smiling, ruddy face and strong right arm impressed more than one young observer during his long career.

JT 'Johnny' Hartwell MC, succeeded Dawe in 1943 and, sadly, died in harness in 1948. *'A large, majestic man, with white hair and a close-clipped white moustache'*, Hartwell may justly be regarded as the father of the twentieth century Hampton sporting tradition. He had nurtured and overseen school games and sports since 1907, except for the Great War years. From 1936 he had dedicated himself to the evolution of the Hanworth Road games fields in preparation for the move in 1939. Old Hamptonians like Stan Holtom attest their gratitude to his wartime organisation

JT Hartwell

of what perforce was a limited sports programme. Yet no-one was allowed to forget that one of the most important responsibilities of a Senior Master was to maintain discipline within the School. In his tribute to Hartwell, Holtom recalls being given *'the whack'* on one occasion by the Senior Master for *'cutting clink'*, that is not going to detention which in his case had been given him by a prefect for *'running in the corridor'*. Holtom goes on:

'It was, therefore, somewhat ironic that I was honoured to attend Johnny Hartwell's funeral as the school representative, escort his coffin and participate in the spreading of his ashes on the football field he built and revered.'

'Jammy' James

Mention has already been made of WD 'Jammy' James' influence in the School. He had served in 1916 as an officer in the South African contingent at Delville Wood on the Somme that left him with shell-shock. He arrived at Hampton in 1921. As well as senior english master at the Grammar School, he was the founding Headmaster and proprietor of Denmead Preparatory School in Wensleydale Road and therefore already well known to numbers of boys who had entered Hampton via the 'Denmead' route.

Mike Tadman describes 'Jammy' James:

'Two eyes like chips of flint looked unflinchingly through a pair of gold-rimmed glasses, beneath a high domed forehead and a bald scalp. His nose came to a point, like a bird's beak, and his lips were a compressed line. He could be literally terrifying when he wished to express displeasure.'

Tadman doesn't recall James smiling or laughing all the time he knew him. However, he says the master was an excellent teacher *'... by the standards of the time, good at explaining things and very fair.'* Dennis Barnes has a down-to-earth

WD James

memory of James as '... *a great teacher but totally politically incorrect with his instructions to pupils to "Stand on your hind trotters, put your snout into your book, and read for us".*

Like Tadman, Barnes, and Franklin, Charles Cleall attests to James' teaching ability:

'He was the biggest influence on my entire intellectual life. He taught us English in Form V, and had us write words we had misspelt, followed by their definition in the sense we had intended, and every aspect of their etymology, with the meaning of that etymology ...Seeing brevity as the soul of wit, Mr James invited us to define Mnemonic. I proffered "Any structural peculiarity whereby a word may be remembered"; which he brushed aside in favour of his own phrase, "A memory trick"... He was not in the least unsympathetic, but succeeded in keeping a cool distance from us all, in unsmiling, unhurried calm, never raising his voice. I don't remember his ever needing to punish anyone.'

Later, we shall observe James' influence in the light of his great passion for ballroom dancing that former pupils remember with delight.

Frank Steffens and Harry Crocker

Mentioned in the same reverential breath as James, by David Franklin and others, were Frank Steffens and 'Harry' Crocker. Both were exempted by the Government from call-up due to their expertise, respectively, in maths and science and importance in the School's ATC unit. Steffens, a former Captain of School, well regarded and affectionately nicknamed 'Stiffneck' by some, was head of maths and taught the most and least able public examinations candidates with equal facility. Not to be trifled with in the classroom, he had a habit of standing at the back of the class, says David Franklin, which enabled him to see whose head was beginning to droop to one side, and then he would be onto his victim like a fox pouncing on a rabbit. His extra-mural contribution was prodigious the year round, at summer camps, in the ATC and on the games field. An easy-going man, his equable nature, though, did not protect him later in the war from a stress related illness.

Harry Crocker was one of Charles Cleall's heroes:

'... I admired my heroes in a way which made me wish to emulate them. Calm, dignified, commanding officer of the cadet force [ATC]: he taught physics in a way which challenged, yet the laughter lines beside his eyes did not deceive. He liked us as much as we liked him and we held him in high respect.'

Of all his colleagues, Crocker was probably the most versatile in the classroom, although his teaching suffered after 1941 due to his frequent absences on ATC business. He taught all three sciences – biology was his greatest love, but he had to wait till after the war to establish it as a Highers course at the School. As George Kerpner remembers, he also taught spanish for a while during a staffing crisis, mugging up his lessons the night before. As we shall see, Crocker played a leading role in the school's Air Training Corps (ATC) that was founded in 1941 and at the end of the war he was awarded an MBE for his services.

'Gassy' Garside

Of those who went into the services in the early years of the war, Bernard Garside was perhaps the most prominent in *'Bossy's old guard'*. Having seen action on the Italian Front in 1918, he joined the staff in 1924. Highly regarded in the academic world for his historical research on the village of Hampton, 'Gassy' (or 'Firpo' or 'Snowball ', a reference to his shock of hair) was an able history teacher and a caring housemaster. He could inspire the loyalty and academic efforts of the games players, as he was one himself. Pat Gubbins was one such sportsman: although no great scholar,

B Garside

he enjoyed history and worked hard for a teacher with whom he had established a rapport. Having had an especially good fortnight in history, Pat was awarded a 'very good' on his grade card by Garside. To mark the occasion, Garside inscribed Gubbins' autograph book with a piece of verse:

> 'The only rhyme for Gubbins
> I can think of is Muggins.
> But that is too hard
> For his fortnightly card
> Shows he has been doing his "scrubbins".'

Garside could, though, turn boys off his subject with his obsession with facts and punctuation. While Ken Skelton thought highly of him, he testifies to Garside the pedant, whose methods included an element of physical coercion to make boys study as he wanted.

> 'Garside had an unfortunate way of giving out his notes. He would wander round the room [dictating] notes which we copied down like mad. As he wandered round he would look over your shoulder and if you didn't get the English right he would slap the back of your head until you put in the little full-stop or some other punctuation. And he would repeat it and your head would bounce up and down until you got the punctuation in.'

'Bill' Yarrow

There was no full-time music master as such at Hampton before or during the war. The outstanding musical talent, for instance, of Thurston Dart who left the Grammar School at the end of the 1930s would have developed in spite of the paucity of formal school music. Yet there were musically qualified staff who were actively devoted to the extra curricular provision of a school choir, recitals, concerts and light opera at the School which went some way to fill a hole in the formal curriculum. WP 'Bill' Yarrow was an excellent musician as well as one of Mason's best teachers. He was also Charles Cleall's other hero:

> 'Tall, cool, bespectacled, sometime sub-organist of Ely Cathedral), [Yarrow] was kind to me, and taught me English for my final term … in Form VI, where I was impressed by his inviting us to contribute to discussion in a way which made us feel that our views deserved to be taken seriously.'

Peter Hodges, like Cleall a keen musician, remembers Yarrow at the School's summer camp at Cholsey in 1943. At the village school where they stayed there was a piano where, one evening, the master was persuaded to play a piece of

Chopin, full of grace notes, which had been found in the piano stool. *'"Haven't seen this for years," complained Yarrow, but played it magically nevertheless.'*

Yarrow had two enemies during the war: rats and Hitler. Barely a year after the completion of the school organ – very much Yarrow's 'baby' and which Cleall later felt so honoured to be allowed to use to practise – the Governors' Minutes recorded a calamity: rats had attacked and eaten sections of the organ's bellows. The Headmaster reassured his Governors: *'The county rat-catcher has the matter in hand.'* It took a while for repairs to be effected. During the summer of 1944, Hitler struck: mercifully, the Yarrow family was spared. Bossy Mason relates:

'One of the early doodle-bugs landed on Mr Yarrow's house in Sunbury early on the morning of 12 August 1944, leaving intact only a few jars of bottled plums and a pailful of pickled eggs! He, his wife and his little daughter had gone to Hermitage, near Newbury, only four days before, to help run the harvest camp there. I can still see Mr Yarrow's face as he read the telegram delivered by the local policeman an hour or so later, grief at the complete destruction of his home alternating with gratitude that his family was with him unharmed.'

'Tank' Titterton

Charisma and eccentricity there was in abundance in the wartime staff-room. Mr CC Titterton, the art and junior geography master, had come back to Hampton and out of retirement in 1939. A Pickwickian figure, about 5ft7½ins tall, with a round, rosy face and benign expression, Titterton's girth earned him his nickname, 'Tank'. He wore a long brown coat the back of which was covered in paint and ink where boys had flicked the brushes or pens when his back was turned. Disconcertingly, he had a swivel eye which gazed in one direction while, says Charles Cleall, *'its peer was keen elsewhere.'* On occasion, recalls Dennis Barnes, he would say, *'"that boy, stand up"'* and three would stand up, *'just to annoy him.'* Jack Wells says: *'You never quite knew who he was looking at. You got hit around the face by a lot of masters then including Tank. But you were never quite sure who he was aiming at, the next boy or you.'* A gifted marine water-colourist, Titterton had trained informally in art in London, his teacher said to be the son of the artist Quiller Orchardson who painted 'Napoleon on the Bellerophon'. Well travelled, he had spent time in South Africa where he fought in the Boer War. He was a *'fascinating'* raconteur: when boys tired of his lessons they got him going on his travels, his hero Lord Nelson, the 'breeding habits of the petunia', or spiritualist beliefs that he said had once rescued him from a potentially fatal illness. There is general agreement that no-one learnt much from Titterton's lessons. *'Tank's idea of art illustrations was what took our fancy in black ink on cartridge paper. I don't know that we ever handled paint,'* says Cleall. Despite CC Titterton's shortcomings, few, however, would have disagreed with Jack Wells' summary of him as *'delightful.'*

'Acky' Ackroyd

There were other masters who, but for the war, would probably have retired by 1940 due to their age and disabilities. RB 'Acky' Ackroyd, as far as is known, is the longest serving member of staff in the 475 year history of Hampton School, retiring in 1946 after 44 years in harness, dying less than three years later. One of his pupils paid tribute to his memory:

'There was, to the last, enough of the boy in the heart of this man to make him quickly accessible to a child's friendship.'

By the war, however, 'Acky' may have run his course. Charles Cleall recalls:

"Acky" Ackroyd was our grey and wispy physics master ... grey in suit and hair; slight stoop, one claw hand extended, the other in his pocket; pebble-lensed; crackly voice, whose sibilants were unusually audible and, ending a word, prolonged as an actual whistle. We liked him immensely, though unsure of the validity of his conviction that liquid paraffin was just the thing for constipation ...'

Despite his hearing aid, other pupils remember him as being very deaf. John Claxton's memory is that *'we perfected the art of ventriloquism. The problem was not laughing. Poor old Ackie Ackroyd knew someone had said something when we all exploded with mirth, but he didn't have the ability to find out who.'*

'Doughnut' Harrison

Eric M 'Doughnut' Harrison[21] was another kindly soul, who taught geography and had been a choral scholar at Christ's College, Cambridge. John Lovesey remembers his sense of humour: *'If I catch the boy who put in chalk a bun on the blackboard thinking it a doughnut he'll be for it.'* However, 'Doughnut' may at times have overstepped the mark in trying to be one of the boys. Moreover, he had an unstable temper and his pupils could be merciless. Provoked, he would lose his temper completely, shouting and *'lashing out with detentions.'* There may have been no volunteers in Mike Tadman's class to the suggestion that someone should test Harrison's reaction, *'in the interests of scientific research'*, by slamming his desk lid, but others remember teasing Harrison and the slamming of desk lids in his presence elsewhere. Shell-shock from his First World War experiences and, later, the loss of a son were probably the underlying causes of Harrison's flare-ups. 'Doughnut' Harrison retired on a disability pension in 1946.

A Controversial Figure: HWT Jago

There was one master for whom fewer of the sources for this account have a kind word. HWT Jago has already been encountered in the Canteen. Cleall recalls:

'He would have made a convincing third member of a trio with Charlie Chaplin and Adolf Hitler, having the same moustache, interestingly similar features, a wild and rocking walk which Charlie Chaplin would have admired, and a zeal for organizing our school dinners which other schools would truly have envied.'

---

21 EM's younger brother, IRS Harrison also taught at Hampton but was called up in 1939, later winning an MC for gallantry.

Indeed Jago seemed well suited to overseeing the Canteen, a disciplinarian with an overbearing personality. Ray Blackwood recalls a remark in an unguarded moment to one of his classes, *'failed the Civil Service Exam so I became a teacher'*, which may confirm the view of more than one of his pupils that he had a chip on his shoulder. Generally unpopular with the boys, Thurston Jago – occasionally referred to as 'Bert' - was regarded by some as a bully, and he used his tongue, with *'a tendency towards sarcasm and gratuitous humiliation'*, to belabour his pupils.

Jago taught french, taking over as head of modern languages from HR Dawe on the latter's retirement. In the memories of former pupils, Jago's competence was sometimes affected by his personality. John Lovesey recognised the bully in him, although remarking that '... *lessons with him were quite enjoyable for those who didn't have the lashing of his tongue* ...' Junior boys seem to have been terrified of him from the outset. Claxton describes him as '*a tyrant'*. A bright, able linguist like David Franklin who had flourished under the sympathetic tutelage of Jammy James and others up the school, failed General Certificate french under Jago.

Once, though, the french master seemed to meet his match. The story was that Jago had taken against one of his middle school pupils, John Rippengal. According to Derek Rippengal, his younger brother, John wasn't scared of anyone. At the end of one french lesson, Jago, using his feared sarcasm, called the boy *'Lord Rippengal'*. John immediately went up to the master's desk and riposted to his face. *'Sir, I am not Lord Rippengal, neither am I Mr Muck'*. Jago apparently never bothered him again.

That, however, was not the end of the Rippengals' experiences at the hands of this complex man. Derek Rippengal says he was later taught Highers french by Jago, also his form master, and had done well by him. However, the younger brother – like the anonymous senior boy who had stolen the plateful of meat rations from under Jago's nose in the shelters - may have excited a certain streak in Jago's nature. Derek Rippengal says he innocently remarked to the french assistant – without first informing Jago – that he had won a place at Cambridge to read Law. Jago took

Headmaster, Mr Jago, Rosemary Jago, Miss Brown

umbrage, scarcely spoke to Rippengal after that and omitted to write his form master's comment on the boy in his final school report.

Dennis Barnes, though, saw another side of Jago:

'A fearsome looking, but gentle man. I copped a detention on one occasion and he had no idea what to do with me. We ended up by sorting his stationery store. Another time Mr Jago was doing dining room duty. That day we were having cold meats and salad, a favourite meal of mine. Unfortunately the only salad dressing the dinner ladies had been able to provide was the oil from sardine cans. At that time of my life I could not eat fish of any description, it made me sick. Mr Jago was able to return my plate to the kitchen and obtain a meal sans sardine oil.'

And during an air-raid, recalls Stan Tanner, *'ole Jago'* was a master of the situation:

'On one occasion, we had just entered the shelter and a string of bombs dropped nearby. The ground shook and of course the boys started to chatter. It was Mr. Jago's French class. He put one foot up on the bench, rattled his change in his trouser pocket and roared, "Quiet! Just because the Hun sees fit to drop a few bombs is no reason to interrupt my French Class! Pay attention!" Nobody laughed but looking back I often chuckle as I think of the audacity of those masters at Hampton.'

Immediately after the war, Thurston Jago, on behalf of the staff, took one of the leading roles in the fight against a local attempt to 'comprehensivise' Hampton Grammar School. He taught at the School until his retirement in 1963.

The 'Sirs': the Mistresses at Hampton Grammar School

If Garside, Mason and the latest history of Hampton School are to be believed, the female teachers – or 'mistresses' or 'lady masters' – who taught at Hampton Grammar during the period 1940 to 1945 were only there as stopgaps for absent conscripted male staff.

Even though the recent history of the school does justice to the important contribution of 'mistresses' to school life in the later twentieth century, it conveys little of their role during the Second World War and does not mention – as Garside does earlier in his history of Hampton School – that six 'mistresses', replacing masters on active service in the First World War, had left after 1918. Garside, however, says almost nothing about the mistresses in his more extensive account of the period between 1939 and 1945. His only reference to 'mistresses' is that there were seven at the school by early 1941. Unintentionally perhaps, Garside belittles by omission the contribution that these and the others made to the wartime school. His Spartan sentiment is revealed:

'Eleven masters on the Staff in January 1947 had been there ... in 1939. Only the Headmaster and they could convey the ethos [Garside italicises 'ethos'] of the pre-war school; so that a dozen men had a heavy responsibility.'

The mistresses get short shrift in Mason's brief history of the School during the Second World War, written as an epilogue to 'Hamptonians at War'. Ironic allusions, à la Garside, to the sanctity of the male preserve abound. In *'... a brief reference to the masters of the staff at the school, all of whom are, of course, are regarded as members of the OHA and part of the School "family" ...',* Mason names certain of the male staff who went off to the war early on. These and others who departed later were, he says, *'replaced by men not fit for active service or, from 1940 onwards, by a succession of ladies, of whom eventually the School had no less than twenty eight, though never more than fourteen at once. The first ladies to arrive came as a batch of four in September 1940. One of these was Miss GR Harrison, who six years later was the last to leave. It is very tempting to write at length about these 'lady masters', usually addressed as 'sir' by the boys, but the title of this book is "Hamptonians at War".'* Finally, Mason says that by the summer of 1945 news had come in about *'... a number of well-loved and respected masters – and even "lady masters" too – who had retired or died.'*

So what impact did the 'mistresses' really make on Hampton? First, the Headmaster had difficulty getting his head round how the 'women' were to be addressed. Several pupils remember him going on at length about this 'problem' in morning assembly. Tadman recalls:

'The only acceptable alternatives, he pointed out, were "Madam", which would make us sound like shop assistants, or "Ma'am", which would sound as though we were addressing the Queen. In the end, he said, the safest thing would be to address all staff, male and female alike, as "Sir".'

To underscore the temporary nature of mistress appointments, the following entry is to be found under *'Miscellaneous'* in the *'Rules Special to War-time Conditions'* in the School's Rule Book for 1942: *'Ladies on the staff may be addressed as 'Miss X', 'Mrs Y' or as 'Sir' – not as 'Miss.'*

'Sir' would include Marjory Brown, his secretary, who reflects with amusement:

'So I became "sir", although ... when the boys were waiting outside my office for various reasons, I used to hear them say, "Is old Maggie in?" I was very amused but I never let on that I had heard. In fact I felt in a way honoured as I believe it was a term of endearment.'

Second, sixty years on, former pupils were in no doubt about the significance of the mistresses' arrival. Mike Tadman, *'the ultimate sensation'*; Charles Cleall, *'the right sort of women, and an excellent group they were'*; and Alan Meacock, comparing them with The Lady Eleanor Holles girls, *'The arrival of mistresses to replace the younger masters was much more exciting.'* Stan Tanner remembers the arrival of the first lady teacher at morning assembly: *'It induced a hum and perhaps rather inelegant whistles which were subdued by the Head immediately.'*

As a group the mistresses tended to fall into two categories: on the one hand, the middle-aged and married, with years of teaching experience. *'I am told these wielded an iron discipline'*, says Alan Meacock. On the other hand, there were, in Meacock's words, *'the young and pretty ones.'*

Tadman speaks for most when he maintains that on the whole the mistresses maintained discipline *'pretty well considering their trying circumstances, apart from a slight tendency to table-rapping and raised voices when things got boisterous.'* Help, though, was not far away for a mistress who was in danger of being given the run around by a class. John Warmington remembers one who left the class in tears. *'Within minutes Mason appeared. By the time he had finished telling us our collective fortunes we felt lower than the knees of a grasshopper.'*

Inevitably, there were one or two of the 'replacement' staff who couldn't cope. The 1941 spring edition of The Lion trumpeted the arrival of a mistress, who happened to be one of the younger ones. Dr AM Baker, an art history teacher *'... who is the daughter of Professor HS Baker, CBE FRS, a gas mask inventor'*, had joined the staff. Unfortunately for the establishment and for Dr Baker, at least one junior class seemed to have no respect for pedigree. Mike Tadman recalls:

'The moment she came in the door we had her marked as a loser. She had only just started the first lesson when someone started playing her up. His name was Edwards, a complete tearaway, always up to some mischief or other. A couple of his cronies joined in. The rest of us just sat back and watched the fun. By the end of the lesson she was almost in tears. She only lasted one term.'

An experienced 'mistress', such as Mrs Wolfe, knew a trick or two that would get her pupils to knuckle down. Mrs Wolfe once turned to her colleague and husband for support concerning one of her fourth form german sets. Dr Wolfe was a formidable schoolmaster who is said to have once played rugby for London Irish. John Lovesey, a member of the german class, relates:

'We were all doing very badly. One day we went into her husband's class – he took us for Chemistry – and he said, "Hands up those boys in the German set". We put our hands up and he said, "You little swine. You are in my wife's German set. If I hear anything about you when I get home it's six of the best in gym shorts by me." Mrs Wolfe taught us to remember things like the words of 'O Tannenbaum' off by heart. We sailed through German and got our matric.'

Another wife and husband presence on the staff were the Crockers. Although not especially striking, says Tadman, Mrs Crocker was tall, broad and oozed authority. *'We came to her class expecting discipline, we got it and we toed the line.'*

Mistresses like Mrs McDermott impressed boys and staff in different ways. An effective teacher of french, Tadman remembers her as *'... a very good-looking woman in a rather hard way. A very snappy dresser, she was beautifully made-up and wore a lot of red which suited her. She always came to work in one of a collection of striking hats.'* Years later Tadman renewed his acquaintance with Bill Yarrow and when they broached the subject of Mrs McDermott, Yarrow roared with laughter: *'Oh God, we were all terrified of her in the staff room.'*

These were able teachers. Miss KL Dickinson made an immediate mark. Clearly a high flier she later went on to become a headmistress. Cleall recalls: *'She taught me English, and was my form-mistress in my first term. She was crisp and terse, somewhat distant, but not unsympathetic ...We all admired and liked her.'* Miss GR Harrison,[22] the longest serving of all the female teaching staff, taught science and geography. *'She was a delight. Petite, round-eyed, high-coloured of cheek, and slightly nervous, she appealed to our protective instincts too much for us to play about in her lessons. She had the knack of letting us do what she wanted.'*

Cleall tells an uncorroborated story about an incident in one of Miss Harrison's lessons. *'I remember Miss Harrison discovering a classmate in possession of a Mauser revolver, and directing him to report with it to Mr*

---

22   Not related to the Harrison brothers

Hartwell. A quick-witted associate asked permission to leave the room, chased after the miscreant, who collaborated in removing part of the weapon, so that what Mr Hartwell saw was evidently harmless, and dismissed as such. This mildly puzzled Miss Harrison when the miscreant returned.'

Miss ML 'Milky' Knight, an historian, was so-nicknamed thanks apparently to a humourist in Ken Skelton's class who appended a Y to her initials which she used after writing notes on the blackboard. She would append 'please leave' and put her initials MLK. She knew what she was about, however, says Cleall. *'Her dark hair, pale face, clipped speech, and brisk manner, helped us to focus on her subject, in which she was so interested that we were too.'*

It was their general contribution to the extra-curricular life of the School as well as in the classroom that marks out the third dimension of the mistresses' impact. There was the oboist, Miss Foreman; 'Milky' Knight ran the current affairs and history clubs; Miss Green put on school plays; and then there was the redoubtable Mrs Wolfe, rated by Robin Bligh as the best of the women who taught him. Mrs Wolfe was a lady of several parts. Charles Cleall remembers her as *'... a tall, well-built matron whose significance to me was that she was not only kindly but a splendid pianist ...'*, who joined him in the 'Three Bears' duet by Eric Coates in one of the School concerts. Like a number of her female colleagues on different occasions, Mrs

Miss ML Knight

Wolfe accompanied the Cholsey camp contingent in the summer holidays of 1943. Described by Peter Hodges as '... *a chef extraordinaire, she produced an unforgettable rabbit stew from the poor bunnies we'd brained with pitchfork handles from an ever diminishing rectangle of cornfield.*'

Old Hamptonians have speculated that it might have been the '*frisson and challenge*' that motivated the younger mistresses to teach at a boys' school. If that were so then both senior and junior boys, on the evidence available, responded to the 'frisson and challenge'. One remembers: '*We were all on tenterhooks to catch a glimpse of them when they first arrived, and report on their attributes in the Prefects Room.*' At least two of the first mistress appointees were well regarded. George Kerpner remembers Miss Knight '*brightening the scene generally*', while John Lovesey reckons that Miss Orton Smith was '*a bit of a dazzler*'. Another former pupil elaborates. One of the youngest of the twenty eight mistresses was, '*... let me say delicately, top heavy and there were stories galore concerning her and another, about competition among the lads as to who could view exposed flesh, at the top end as well as the bottom end. They would get up to all sorts of ruses like dropping a piece of chalk or visiting the desk.*'

Stan Holtom remembers that the school captain, '*... was obviously smitten by the demeanour of one lady teacher in particular or maybe the vibes went in the opposite direction – but who were we as first formers to know the difference.*'

One anonymous Old Hamptonian goes further: '*Presumably [the younger mistresses] were considered beyond the sexual reach of even the senior boys. If that was the official view I can now reveal that it was mistaken ... One of the young mistresses was "seeing" a Sixth Former out of school and the pair came round to the house of the Sixth Former's friend.*'[23]

We shall never know what Bossy Mason was 'tempted' to write about his lady 'sirs'. It was unfortunate that both he and Garside said so little about them in their pieces on wartime Hampton Grammar School.[24] Perish the thought that this was the ungrateful reaction of a male preserve under threat, but they were writing some time after the 'mistresses' had got together and endowed an annual school 'Mistresses' Prize', as a tribute to the 'masters' who went off to the war and all of whom survived.

---

23   The anonymous Old Hampton contributor says that it was his house they visited. He is unwilling to identify his friend out of respect for his widow.

24   See Postscript below

The Prefects

If wartime circumstances temporarily re-introduced 'mistresses' to the Hampton staff-room, so too these circumstances affected the rôle of the more senior students in the school routine. As the Headmaster might have put it, the Hanworth Road school was a new theatre of operations. By 1941 the war was affecting everyone's lives, the brigadier had been deprived of most of his key officers and he had to depend more than ever on his NCOs to help 'run the show'.

In the front line were the prefects. Mike Tadman, himself never a prefect, recalls:

'The school was run by the prefects. They rang the bells (they had a rota for this); they policed the corridors and the cloakrooms at the start of the day; and were responsible for good order generally ... The prefects were a remarkable body of young men. They performed their duties punctiliously, while never abusing their authority. Since small boys are usually naturally rebellious and resentful of any sort of discipline, it is interesting to recall that the prefects were held in genuine respect – indeed, some of them were almost hero-worshipped.'

John Lovesey's view is that the prefects were *'like gods'*. Prefects had the authority to give detentions and used it. Pat Gubbins remembers being given 'clink' (a detention) by Digger King for 'running in the corridor'. On another occasion, King kept the whole school in for talking after the bell had been rung at the beginning of assembly, Gubbins' class being taken for that detention next day by Jack Knight.

Digger King

Perhaps the most prominent of all the Captains of School during the war was Jack Knight, who held office in 1940 and 1941. Tadman says of him: *'His most visible duty was to marshal and supervise the morning assembly prior to the arrival of Bossy and the staff. This he did from Bossy's rostrum, with skill and efficiency. He was only eighteen years old, but we boys regarded him with awe.'* The summer 1941 edition of The Lion paid tribute: *JB Knight was the only School Captain to be mobbed on the last day of* term for his autograph. He was the first to go straight into the RAF for training. He was a very good School Captain and all wished him "good luck". Like his predecessor Digger King – who was drowned when the ship taking him to a posting in the Sudan was torpedoed – and successor Dick Rudkin, Jack Knight would not survive his active service, dying in November 1943 when he failed to return from a training flight over the Irish Sea.

Jack Knight
(Betty Knight)

The Captain of School from 1943 to 1944 was Michael Brudenell who discusses his rôle in his autobiography. Brudenell believes his appointment as Captain of School in 1943 by the Headmaster was against the wishes of some of the staff, '...who quite understandably resented my big-headedness.' He goes on:

'The rôle of the school captain in 1943 was important in maintaining with his school prefects, school discipline and acting as a liaison between the Headmaster and the boys. There was a weekly prefects' meeting chaired by the school captain; the minutes of these meetings, often edited and expurgated, were passed to the Headmaster for his comments. These were not always complimentary, but I think he welcomed the contact. All the boys of whatever seniority had to wear a school cap to school. The school captain's cap was that of a senior prefect but with gold piping. In 1943 it carried the stamp of authority ... The school captain rang the bell to silence the five hundred boys at

Dick Rudkin

Michael Brudenell
(David Franklin)

Assembly and then greeted the headmaster and staff as they took their places on the stage. I loved every moment of that year but the additional duties ate further into the time I could devote to my exam preparation ...'

Brudenell was certainly a busy young man, in school sports teams, the ATC, his local scout troop in Ashford, in public speaking contests, and as Form, House and eventually School Captain. While he won the Fitzwygram Prize, awarded on a vote by boys and 'masters' [sic] at the end of his final summer term, for the most meritorious contribution to the School, he encountered problems, as he says, with his academic commitment. In addition to his Highers courses he had also to work for the first examination for the degree of MB BS for entry into King's College Medical School. While all was well eventually, he failed first time round, passing only biology which he had had to study with the girls over at The Lady Eleanor Holles because Hampton did not offer biology at Highers level.

It wasn't all hard slog for the prefects. A traditional annual perk that they enjoyed was their prefects' social at the end of the summer term – and not least the 'Liquid Refreshment' that was surreptitiously conjured up at the end. Organised by the staff, there were songs and music hall turns and musical chairs. If musical chairs, played by hefty 17 and 18 year olds was insufficiently energetic, then the rugby match that followed in one of the gyms was of a different order. Jammy James was the referee, but it was said that he would only blow his whistle before someone was seriously injured.

Captains of School

1938-9	J. STEEDMAN (B).
1939-0	D. G. KING (B).
1940-1	J. B. KNIGHT (B) (to Apr. 41).
1941-2	R. C. RUDKIN (B) (Apr. 41 to Oct. 41).
	J. E. NEWELL (B) (Oct. 41 to July 42).
1942-3	J. D. EMERSON (P).
1943-4	J. M. BRUDENELL (G).
1944-5	M. I. COUTTS (B) (to Sept. 30th. 44).
	A. A. H. CLARKE (P) (Oct. 1st. to 7th. 44).
	A. C. S. BROWN (B) (Oct. 8th. 44 to June 25th 45).
	J. F. S. FRITH (B) (June 26th 45 to end July).
1945-6	W. L. PARKER (P) (to Dec 45).
	E. A. RAYNHAM (W) (Jan to July 45).
1946-7	J. M. SUTTON (B).

Cupid darts across the Fence

Prefects' perks were as nothing, however, to the 'frisson' created by innovatory inter-school activities for more senior Hampton and Holles pupils. As we have already discovered, on the one hand some of the boys were fascinated by certain of their 'mistresses'. However, the cheek-by-jowl proximity of the two schools offered different and scarcely resistible challenges to Hampton boys - as well as, presumably, to The Holles girls. Several of the reminiscences and memoirs still betray the awkwardness of adolescence. Michael Brudenell declares: *'The sporting activity made for a very limiting social life. When I read of the social and sexual activities of that age today, I seem by comparison to have led the life of a monk!'* Notwithstanding his favourable views concerning the advent of mistresses at Hampton, Alan Meacock, adjudging himself a *'slow developer'*, muses on the *'... voyeurship ...'* through the school fence. *'If your form room looked out towards LEH you could become disturbed by the shapely bodies next door playing their field games.'* Peter Mills and his friends had more practical solutions to the problem. They organised games of cricket near The Lady Eleanor Holles fence during the lunch breaks: *'The idea was to hit the ball over the fence in the hope of meeting one of the young ladies who might throw it back. Strangely, I do not remember this being frowned upon. In any case, we met the girls on the bus going home.'* Having to study biology over at The Holles gave Michael Brudenell a much envied contact with the girls. Yet, *'... although I found some of the girls in the Biology class very attractive, I was too busy to get involved – even when I got a Valentine card and the sender appeared at my home during the holidays to "lend me her Biology notes", I still didn't get the message.'*

Mr James, a devotee of ballroom dancing, came up with a memorable solution to the boy/girl problem: dancing classes. George Kerpner offers a retrospective appreciation of the nature of the beast facing the two schools: that ballroom dance lessons for adolescents under strict supervision were introduced to curb the *'primeval behaviour of pubescent boys'* and *'more forward girls'* under the shelter of the trees in the apple orchard near the Longford River that formed the boundary between The Holles and Hampton Grammar. The Headmaster and Headmistress gave the nod and the sessions were to be held on Thursdays after school.

On the appointed afternoon, the girls arrived at Hampton with their chaperones and sat in a single line on one side of the School hall and the boys sat on the other.

Kerpner remembers what happened when the music started:

'We had been told to approach the ladies unhurriedly, yet we knew we had to beat a dozen rivals, so that our artificially retarded sprint must have looked very comical. However, Mr James made sure that all favours were equally distributed as evenly possible, whilst Miss Nicholls, the Headmistress, always seemed to turn up next to you when you had just about got close enough to your partner to feel her sweet breath on your face. She would cruelly pull you apart with a swift and determined jerk, accompanied by a mocking stare. I am sure she enjoyed her part as much as the lovelorn couples did theirs, as they floated past stiffly, or simply stumbled along to the recorded music of Victor Sylvester and his Ballroom Orchestra, slow ... slow ... quick, quick, slow ...'

Brudenell seemed less coy and more calculating on these occasions, not as monkish as he proclaims elsewhere in his autobiography:

'The prettiest girls were quickly snapped up leaving the laggards to dance with the dumplings. I always chose the same girl who was not particularly pretty but who was interested in learning to dance. She put up with having her feet trodden on and between us we mastered the basic steps of the dances, an essential qualification if one was to attend the school dances held at the end of term ... For me and my friends in 1943 the whole thrill of dancing was the opportunity it gave to put your arms around the girl and do the steps together holding her as close as she would allow. Some of the girls wanted to be closer than others but that was about as far as it went.'

Alan Meacock maintains there were no official shared activities and only a rare shared function during his time at the School, the ballroom dancing classes commencing after he left. There may have been more official contact between the two schools than he remembers. Joint concerts and religious services were held. There had been a late afternoon dance initiated by the Headmistress of The Lady Eleanor Holles in February 1941 which involved Hampton boys and 25 of her girls. However, the highlight of that afternoon – according to the summer 1941 Lion – was apparently not the dancing, but an *'amazing'* wartime school tea put on by one of the Canteen ladies.

Nevertheless, the dancing classes began in Meacock's last year and he himself was The Lion's reporter on another innovation involving the two schools: a joint Hampton – Holles sports day in the summer term of 1942. Alan Meacock writes disparagingly about sports day, and the conduct of some senior boys and girls – he refers to them as *'... philandering enthusiasts who leapt at the opportunity like cats to milk.'* He doubts the establishment view that *'all the boys and girls desired the sports.'* *'I believe,'* he wrote in The Lion, *'that the Holles prefects en bloc, not being of a social nature, would have kept out of it which they were not easily permitted to do.'*

He reserves his sharpest arrows for the mixed organising committee, the majority of whom *'behaved like 10 year olds at a Christmas Party.'* The main objective of the committee seemed to be the *'avoidance of responsibility',* for which *'we, the prefects were to blame'. 'It was a pity,'* he says, *'that nine or ten boys and girls are not capable of meeting together, theoretically for serious business, without wasting their time in proving how conceited they are.'* He recorded, though, that Mr James, whose idea it was, thought the occasion a success. In the event, more than 800 people turned up for the sports and side-shows, although the latter realised only £4 for war charities.

Meacock now believes that the flexibility of staff at both schools had enabled the relationship between staff and pupils to become less formal. However, he has vivid and mildly resentful memories of what might be described as 'The Bathroom Door Affair', during his last term in the autumn of 1942:

'Each year forms were encouraged to carry out schemes in aid of war-time charities. I persuaded 6A to put on ... a long sketch called "The Bathroom Door", depicting a Boarding House where there is a growing queue of frustrated guests waiting to get into the bathroom to perform their ablutions ... We planned to present this masterpiece in the school hall and charge the rest of the school good money to see it. The great draw was the cast. There were two female parts and we managed to persuade two LEH girls to play these. This was indeed breaking new ground, and in retrospect I am surprised that Mason agreed to let us do it.

Due to an unfortunate oversight we did not tell anyone about the dress rehearsal, which took place on a Sunday afternoon, and required us to wear dressing gowns over night attire. In the middle of this the caretaker's wife turned up, gave a blood-curdling shriek, and ran for her life. Early on the Monday morning I, as the instigator, was called before Mason. He was glacial in his displeasure. All my excuses were swept aside. At that very moment, he informed me, the LEH girls concerned were being interviewed by Miss Nicholls, their headmistress, and the message to them was the same as to me: not a word must get out about our Sunday rehearsal. Otherwise the reputation of the two schools would be irretrievably ruined. Reluctantly he would allow the production to go ahead, as it was committed. Although I was suitably crestfallen, I was also flabbergasted. How, in the middle of the War could a peccadillo like this create such consternation? Surely there was a lack of balance?'[25]

---

25   Alan Meacock now sees it as a joke, reminiscing that barely two years later he was in action as a young infantry officer on the battle fields of Holland and Germany. Not surprisingly, the sketch's review in The Lion does not mention his confrontation with the Headmaster, only that the sketch went down well with a large audience.

A Sporting War

The indirect consequences of the war were far more disruptive of the development of the School after 1939 than the threat of the Luftwaffe and Hitler's 'secret weapons'. The grounds of Hampton Grammar School, as we have seen, had undergone a series of metamorphoses that before September 1939 would have been beyond the imagination of anyone connected with the future development of the new site. For several years posses of boys and staff had been galvanised to help prepare the fine sports fields and other open spaces that the new School site would provide. However, in less than a year, the area to the front of the School was disfigured by the air-raid shelters, while a patchwork quilt of 120 pits had been dug by the army, wrecking the harmony of the playing fields, with football pitches and cricket squares squeezed between these deterrents to an air-borne landing.

Since the late nineteenth century, the School had built up and keenly maintained a sports tradition for which it was locally renowned. In these very difficult times, especially between 1939 and 1941 and in 1944, it wasn't just tradition that mattered. Schoolboy morale, integral to wartime civilian morale, could be bolstered by the fun, fitness, skill and teamwork derived from sports activities as well as from Bossy's PWD, or 'Public Works Department', harvest camps, the ATC and the Scouts. And sooner rather than later, a war had to be fought and all Hampton Grammar schoolboys, 'mens sana in corpore sano', were in theory liable for active service in His Majesty's armed forces.

School sport could be more easily maintained in schools where facilities and staff were less disrupted by state logistics, defence measures and conscription. Independent and state senior schools, away from dangerous areas, might be more able to maintain extra-curricular sports programmes than others. However, Hampton Grammar – lying in a Government-designated 'neutral' zone but re-located just as war broke out – was immediately confronted not only with the prospect of dismembered playing fields but also with the future of these facilities being jeopardised by a wartime shortage of staff, finance and materials. There was only so much that Bossy Mason's PWD pupil work squads could do to help. Turf on the new fields had scarcely taken root by September 1939 and, as we have already noted, the Royal Engineers would soon be at work to deter the enemy.

WL Parker   PJ Watts   BL Nightingale   JN Stonell
AA Meacock   MM Sharp   LV Woollett   DH Eastland   MI Coutts
JF March   JCL Clarke

Physical education lessons were enhanced by two ultra-modern indoor gymnasia and provided a continuity in weekly exercising that the state of the outdoor amenities and the weather could not always guarantee. JD Simms' PE classes, for instance, seemed the epitome of energy. However, as the Headmaster related in his Notes for The Lion, one neutral observer doubted the wisdom of Simms' efforts. Once, when the PE master ventured outside with a *'lively'* fifth form to organise an obstacle race, a man working on a nearby air-raid shelter pondered:

'Blimey. Marvellous, ain't it? No wonder there's so many cat burglars.'

The School's playing facilities were re-organised to cope with restrictions. However, their usefulness was limited by the evacuation of many other schools on the sports fixture lists. Of the football fixtures, only Isleworth Grammar and the Old Hamptonians survived in 1940 and 1941: one of the 1st XI's ad hoc fixtures was against Hampton First Aid Post. The bitter first winter of the war and the limited provision of external air-raid shelters cut heavily into the programme. Was the unidentified *'Twickenham schoolboy'* contributor to Norman Longmate's 'How We Lived Then' an Old Hamptonian, who recalled that, '... *the lines of pits were fun to play in for younger boys, although annoying in winter if one had to retrieve a football from several inches of mud and water at the bottom.'*?

The popularity of football and the survival of house fixtures through thick and thin were unquestionably assisted by the indefatigable efforts of members of staff like JT Hartwell. The season of 1941 – 1942 saw an increase in the number of schools played, with five XIs fielded on occasion. The ATC more than made up for the inter-school fixture difficulty by organising a full programme of keenly contested matches with other units. It was not until 1944 that the quality and quantity of football at the School returned to its pre-war standards, with more schools re-appearing on the fixture list. Even so, the 1st XI still did not have a full-time coach, and masters continued to take charge of more than one school team.

Athletics customarily occurred in the latter part of the spring term. In 1940, a backlog of house matches, 'THAT MAN', and inadequate preparation of the athletics track intruded, despite the best efforts of the groundsman Pat Verth, Harry Crocker and others. Athletics, however, was not the most favoured of sporting activities. Rarely, reports The Lion, was there a turn-out of more than fifteen runners and on sports day only the School and a few guests were present. This was a scenario that was to be repeated in 1941: again, a poor turn-out on sports day, for which only a limited programme of events could be organised.

651 SQUADRON A.T.C. ATHLETIC TEAM.
WINNERS OF THE S. MIDDLESEX & MIDDLESEX ATHLETIC SPORTS 1944.

WAKEFIELDS EALING 1000

R. Dow.   K. D. Gould.   D. J. Osborne.   F/O. Wolfe.   R. J. Dow.   W. L. Parker.   R. Millard.   D. L. Black.
(Sports Officer).   (Recorder).

O. R. Pugh.   M. I. Coutts.   M. K. Wing.   D. H. Eastland.   I. H. L. Smith.   K. C. Edwards.   V. Mays.
(Captain).

Boxing Ring in the School hall
(Ron Keevil)

It was recorded – undoubtedly at the behest of a Headmaster with a penchant for statistics – that in the last six weeks of the spring term 293 boys, '... *took no advantage whatever of facilities for games that the School affords ... How creditable these figures are to the School as a whole its members can judge for themselves.*'

Yet by 1942, athletics seemed back on track with a full programme of sports day events, while the image of athletics seemed transformed by the first joint HGS – LEH sports day. While we have observed its impact in another direction, the huge attendance from the two schools, at 6d a 'watcher', boosted the Borough of Twickenham's 'Aid to Russia Week'. In the summer of 1943, again the Grammar and The Holles had combined for a summer sports day. Rain, however, curtailed the races, so plays and sideshows in the School hall and cloisters acted as useful diversions for the young patrons. The only disenchanted participant seems to have been the School Captain who, having been the target of a '*vicious enfilading fire of tennis balls*' at the Aunt Sally, expressed the hope that he would have left the school before next year's occasion.

The School's cricket fixtures, mostly against schools similarly sited in a 'neutral' zone, were enthusiastically pursued to the end of the summer term of 1940, despite the beginning of Luftwaffe bombing in June. The number of low-scoring innings suggests that cricket squares were much less well prepared than they had been a year previously. This suited the talents of a 15 year old Hamptonian bowler, Pat Gubbins – already playing for both the 2nd and 1st XIs – who recorded in his diary a tally of 44 wickets in 14 matches. The cricketers did not seem to be put off if the war intruded, as we have already learned from a Gubbins diary entry for that July.

A shortage of equipment, not least of cricket balls, bedevilled cricket throughout the war, yet the premier of school team sports was avidly maintained for the duration. Four XIs were fielded on occasion and, as with football, a full programme of house matches was played each summer. Only the intervention of the flying bomb in the summer of 1944 disrupted fixtures to any extent – half had to be cancelled.

Boxing, like football, flourished at house level as well as in the ATC and had a grand new arena in the School hall. Before the war two Old Hamptonian doctors had donated a ring and it was put to popular use on numerous occasions. *'House boxing was tremendous,'* remembers John Lovesey, *'The hall was full to overflowing for the 1941 tournament. The Blitz was still on and if anything had happened there were 700 people in the hall watching the boxing ... !'*

It was not until after the war, however, when masters returned and the fields were put to rights – and then only after a dispute between the Governors and the War Office as to who was to pay for their restitution – that all the School's sports, including the swimming gala, were properly reconstituted.[26]

School Music

Music-making does not feature as an important Hampton Grammar School subject or extra-mural activity in Mason's 'Russia Account' in June 1945. The Headmaster deposits it in his 'Miscellaneous' section on extra-mural activities. There had been no music master before or during the war; and music, otherwise known as class singing, appeared in the timetable of only forms one and two. No provision could thus be made for a boy to take study GSC music at the School. Pre-war music making had very much involved members of staff, especially in the Gilbert and Sullivan productions and the 'End of Term Entertainment', both activities disappearing after the summer of 1939 for the duration of the war.

Did Mason have as one of his goals for the new school the creation of a music tradition at Hampton Grammar School? Certainly the Governors had provided impressive facilities to work with – the new school hall, a pipe organ and a Bechstein grand piano. The onset of war could, of course, be blamed for the-long term disruption of a goal. Yet, a post of music master was not created for

---

26   The first School swimming gala after 1939 was held at the local pool at the end of July 1945

September 1939, in anticipation of such a goal, and it was some years after the war before a full-time music master was appointed.

Thanks to the musically gifted, enthusiastic and over-worked Bill Yarrow and Eric Harrison, music was kept alive at Hampton during the war. The hosting of the annual south-west Middlesex Music Festival in the hall in the summer term of 1940, in which LEH also participated, provided the School with an ideal showcase for its musical ambitions. The facilities may have impressed, but while there were promising solo performances from the violinist, David Channon, and a third form treble, FB Wedgwood who sang 'How beautiful are the feet' from The Messiah, the School Choir merely made do with the stirring, but unambitious Ralph Vaughan Williams composition, 'Let us now praise famous men'. Even so, the South-West Middlesex Music Festival was an annual event, held in different venues, and Hampton Grammar was always represented, notwithstanding the patchy quality of the School's music. Those who attended the 1943 event, though, must have been thrilled by the presence of one of Britain's finest twentieth century composers, Dr Ralph Vaughan Williams, as conductor of the Festival orchestra.

There was no school orchestra in those days so Yarrow and Harrison concentrated on the choir. Early on it was about 70 strong and performed at festivals that were attended by – amongst others – the choir of Twickenham County Grammar School for Girls. Singing may not have been the only draw-card for Hampton choristers. Admitting to having a Twickenham County girlfriend at the age of 11, John Lovesey says, *'We were most interested in [them] and they in us.'* The star Hampton chorister at the time was the outstanding treble, FB Wedgwood, while after 1942 the Choir enjoyed the voice of Charles Cleall, who had joined the school for his examination years and was already an accomplished organist. The choir could also draw on the experience and abilities of a number of boys singing in their local church choirs, including the Chapel Royal, Hampton Court Palace. The Headmaster and Governors, however, seemed indifferent to a need to encourage choral music making in and out of the School. Chorister absence for extraordinary church services during school time was seen as disruptive of classroom routine. It is sad that the admonishment handed down from the Governors and Headmaster in July 1942, ' ... *the absence of choir boys ... for special church services is contrary to school rules*', was the sole recorded comment in Governors' Meetings during the war on cultural education at the School.

The advent of two excellent 'mistress' musicians, Miss Foreman and Mrs Wolfe, enhanced individual music-making, as Cleall has attested. Six boys and staff gave a well received recital to the Music Society during the autumn of 1943. The Society met regularly later on, with Mr Short, a Cambridge maths master, in charge and helped by pupil classical music lovers like DH Warner and Derek Rippengal.

A Festival of JS Bach's music, held in connection with the 'Holidays at Home' scheme in the summer of 1942, was the most innovative event held at the School during the war. Although the school choir performed, their choice of piece, a Parry setting of an extract from Richard II titled 'England', was unadventurous. Moreover, the reviewer commented on the sparseness of attendance and that the atmosphere that afternoon was spoilt by the inattentiveness of *a certain minority in the audience who whispered during a piano duet featuring Mrs Wolfe and Mr Yarrow.'* Two years later, a report on the Music Society in The Lion got closer to the malaise affecting music at the School. While there was praise for an individual performer like Charles Cleall, the reporter reflected on attending or performing at Society meetings and school concerts. *'Either there is an astonishing lack of musical talent in the school, or a pronounced shyness where playing before an audience is concerned.'* In expressing appreciation to the jazz enthusiasts who attended Society gatherings, the reporter, without tongue in cheek, also revealed the rudder-less parochialism of Hampton's music: *'We would like to show our gratitude by promising them a meeting before the end of term devoted to "this kind of music".'*

The Home Front …

By 1941, as the threat of invasion had begun to recede, the war-effort at the School was now about 'making do', *'Don't You Know There's A War On?'*, and helping the war effort by *'Digging For Victory'*. The brigadier Headmaster had become a colonial administrator, as ever the 'Public Works Department' enthusiast. A Garden Club was formed; allotments were constructed in between the air-raid shelters and on other spare ground, cared for by up to 50 boys; poultry runs were erected, to be cared for by the School Poultry Club; and a couple of bee-hives were placed in the farther recesses of the School property, overseen by the Bee Club. These, together with the School's wartime summer harvest camps so popular with boys in the middle and upper school, had re-created an awareness of agricultural life which was reflected in the new and increasingly well-attended School's Young Farmers' Club. Not least in the annals of pupil and staff support for the war effort was the major increase in voluntary financial contributions to campaigns, such as the 'Wings for Victory' week in the spring of 1943 and the 'Salute the Soldier' week a year later. The Grammar School itself was the beneficiary of a gift from a former parent of £375 in Defence Bonds, the largest single donation to the School, in the opinion of the Headmaster, *'since 1692'*.

... and the Pig Club

The war-effort spawned one civilian extra-curricular activity at the School that previously would have been beyond the ken of even the Headmaster and his great enthusiasm for 'Public Works': the Pig Club. By the summer of 1945 the club had achieved fame, notoriety and success in unequal measure. The government of the Soviet Union was told of the Hampton Grammar School Pig Club by the Headmaster in a specially commissioned account on the School. The Pig Club had been decorated with the motto, *'Per Ardua ad Cibum'*, by the waggish editors of The Lion;[27] while from its inception in March 1942, the Pig Club's devotees had laboured to guarantee a small, but regular supply of porkers for the nation's food supply.

In the context of nation-wide wartime food production, it should be said that the School's Pig Club was by no means unique. Pig stocks on farms nation-wide during the war actually fell by more than a half, due to the need to save on imported foodstuffs. Urban pig-keeping proliferated in consequence, actively encouraged by the Government. Norman Longmate relates: *'There were pig clubs on school playing fields, in open spaces like Battersea Park and even in the swimming-bath of the bombed out Ladies Carlton Club in Pall Mall.'*

Unsurprisingly, the paragraph on the Pig Club in the Headmaster's 'Russia Account' is bland to a degree. Mason betrays none of the secrets of its vicissitudes, nor indeed risks guffaws at the Home Office by revealing that the club conducted its activities behind the bike sheds.

---

27   A parody of the RAF motto, 'Per Ardua ad Astra'. 'Cibum' = 'food'

'The Pig Club consists of two masters and about 30 boys. It was begun as a war-time measure, primarily to avoid waste of food and to increase the meat supply. The members built their own pig sties and bought their own equipment. Of each pair of pigs killed one is sold to the Ministry of Food and the other is shared among the members, who pay for the meat at the normal prices. The members feed and look after the pigs. The waste food from the [school] kitchen is used for pig food after being boiled. The club breeds its own pigs.'

The reality of the Pig Club's wartime history was much more complicated. Despite Mason's retrospective description of the Club in his 'Russia Account', its existence is never once acknowledged in the minutes of Governors' meetings during the war, and there is no record of any funds made available from the School for the construction of the sties.

Moreover, there is ambiguity concerning the creation and running of the Pig Club. According to the recollections of former sixth former Stan Tanner, the driving force behind the creation of the Pig Club was Tanner himself. As we have already seen elsewhere, he had definite ideas about the nutritional value of school food. He recalls that from an early age, he had nursed ambitions of becoming a vet. What better way of harnessing the disposal of the school dining room's waste food output to the war-effort by starting a pig club. He went to see the Headmaster. Bossy Mason thought it a good idea, that Tanner would be credited *'for devising the plan'* but that he Tanner would be *'entirely responsible for running a Pig Club'* and would bear the consequences should he fail to follow the scheme through. Stan Tanner accepted the responsibility. However, a member of staff had to act as an *'advisor'*. The Head suggested Bill Yarrow. Whether Yarrow had previously been consulted by Mason is unclear – Yarrow had been away from school, still recovering from a bout of pneumonia. Tanner thereupon visited Bill Yarrow at his home in Sunbury. The master was confined to bed and his wife ushered the sixth former into the bedroom.

'I stood at the foot of the bed, cap in hand. Bill's long artistic fingers grasped the top of the sheet under his chin. His wan face recorded his recent bout of illness.

"Hello, Tanner, it is good of you to call".

"Sir, you have been elected President of the Pig Club".

For a moment there was a startled silence. Then he sat bolt upright in bed and said, "President of the what?"'

By what process Yarrow had been 'elected' is not known – perhaps 'elected' should read 'by Headmaster's fiat'. Yarrow therefore became President, an 'advisory' post for which he was not completely unqualified as he had grown up on a farm.

Thus, whereas Mason implies in his 'Russia Account' that it was the School's initiative that set up the Pig Club, Stan Tanner claims that it was his. Mason says that the Pig Club had a master in charge, Tanner claims that Yarrow's role as 'President' was advisory. Tanner, though, does not mention that 'Jammy' James was the Pig Club's treasurer. Tanner's version that the Headmaster would hold him personally responsible for the creation and administration of a Pig Club is at odds with the legal responsibility the School had for its pupils' permitted activities within its aegis. Extraordinarily, however, the Governors had already compromised their legal position a year earlier towards out-of-school activities, by refusing to accept responsibility 'in case of accidents that might occur'.[28]

White Yorkshire boar

'Per Ardua ad Cibum' was an apt motto for the Pig Club. Providing pork for the nation's food supply was indeed a struggle. Whereas Stan Tanner's account of the politicking behind the running of the Pig Club is related from the safety of the early 21st century, his epic on the provision of the sty, between the bike sheds and the Rectory fence, is from The Lion of summer 1942. At first there was difficulty in obtaining materials for the sty's construction.

Our first help came from Mr Hamlin, Superintendent of the Refuse Disposal Works in Hanworth Road. He lent us some timber to construct moulds for reinforced concrete walls. E Fuller (6a) went to a great deal of trouble to get us 10cwt of cement and a load of ballast. Then we started to erect a wall. It was a wall fit to keep out an army when we removed the boarding. Proudly we displayed it to Mr Yarrow, who occupied the post of adviser [sic]. He touched it – and it fell over! For fifteen minutes we roared with laughter. Payne placed an iron maul on the middle of the slab, and it [the concrete] bent in the middle! More laughter and "I told you so" from Mr Yarrow. Again Fuller came to the rescue, with one hundred and fifty breeze blocks and five sheets of asbestos [!] roofing ... Now the sty was nearly finished ... If anyone thinks the sty looks amateurish, let him start from scratch and build

28   See below

one next to it at the expense of £8, blistered hands and a large amount of ridicule from small boys.'

Running the sty was a test of endurance. Removing manure and preparing swill for the pigs was a thankless, odiferous task. Each evening the swill, mostly from the kitchens of both the Grammar and The Holles, would have to be boiled up for two hours, with bran supplied each month by the Government (thanks to the Club's membership of the Small Pig Keepers Association of Great Britain from the autumn of 1942). The pigs were also fed with inedible potatoes from the school allotments and elsewhere: these would have been 'clamped' in an adjacent plot, that is, placed under straw to protect them from the weather.

Then there were distractions. Younger members of the Club could be diverted from their duties. Less well-intentioned friends might use an occasion to visit the pigs for laddish behaviour. The clamped potatoes were irresistible. One afternoon after school John Warmington and a friend, Geoff Collins, accompanied two other friends, Terry Blunt and Tony Van Toll who were members of the Pig Club, to the pig sty behind the cycle sheds, where they engaged in a potato-throwing fight. The groundsman spotted them and next morning in assembly Bossy Mason announced that the four boys involved in a potato fight – *'I know who they are'* – should report to the study forthwith. Waste as well as ill-discipline easily incurred the wrath of the Headmaster. Warmington remembers what happened next:

'"You are not a bad boy, Warmington," said the Headmaster, "But if you break the rules you must expect to be punished – bend over." The Headmaster laid six strokes of his cane on my backside. Really hurt!'

The pigs, naturally, were capable of even greater ill-discipline and could not be caned for it. The Lion reported in the spring of 1944 that the President's coat, left on the sty railing, was *'chewed (in real American fashion)'* by two of the inhabitants but rescued before any serious damage was done. If the pigs managed to escape, the chips were down. Joan Styan, in the BBC's 'WW2 People's War', recalls her husband Peter's account of his experience:

'One fateful Sunday, when it was his turn to feed the pigs, he discovered, to his horror, that the gate of the pig-sty had been left unlatched and all the pigs had fled. After much searching, he finally caught up with them after cycling around the school fields and managed patiently to shepherd them back to the sty. They were actually next to a gate leading on to the road. He was so relieved as he would have been held responsible for their loss.'

Mayhem was never far away, as Stan Tanner remembers:

'On Christmas Day 1942 about midday the Headmaster telephoned my house and said that there were six pigs in line ahead, proceeding along Wensleydale Road.

They were presently in an irate houseowner's garden looking for goodies. Once again, the fellow on duty had failed to latch the gate to the pen securely. Christmas afternoon was spent with a couple of other HGS seniors driving the pigs back to the school and their pen. My father came along too. Evidently the pigs recognized the full weight of the law and complied with our efforts.[29]

Even worse, The Lion reported in the autumn of 1943, was the *'consternation'* caused when on one occasion *'one of the younger porkers escaped and got into the school.'* No names, no pack drill – but a 'younger porker'? Stan Tanner fills in the details. One morning, during his last months at the School, he was summoned from Mr Crocker's chemistry class by the Headmaster.

'I went immediately to the Head's study. Lying across the study door was the largest sow we had. Maybe she wanted to absorb some education for her piglets!

"What is that, Tanner?"

Well, if he didn't recognise a pig who was I to but.

"It's a pig, sir."

"Yes, Tanner, put it back where it belongs!"

I was getting off light I was -----

"Then come back and see me!"

After a lecture on the responsibility and management of pig club members who might neglect to latch the pen after feeding the pigs, I was released and returned to the chemistry lab.'

... and the Allotments

The School was curiously luke-warm towards its allotment scheme. Useful for the production of vegetables for the school dining room, the summer harvest camps, as well as for home tables, the scheme came into being in the summer of 1941. In July, in the first – and last – reference to the allotments in the minutes of Governors' meetings during the war, the Headmaster's recommendation that fifty allotments should be set aside for cultivation by boy plot-holders, between the main school and the Hanworth Road, was accepted

---

29   Tanner's father was a policeman

by the Governors. However, the boys were *'to supply their own tools'*, supervision was to be *'only general'*, and the Headmaster and Governors would not accept *'responsibility, in case of accidents that might occur'*. Furthermore, after three years of productive endeavour and no actionable accidents, the motivation of the allotment tillers was unfairly dismissed by the Headmaster in his 'Russia Account': *'About 40 or 50 boys cultivate for their own private amusement and gain, small plots of land near the main building.'* No mention here of the seasonal supply of vegetables to the school dining room and summer harvest camps. No wonder, then, that the allotments and the Pig Club, from their inception, received such ambiguous support from the Headmaster and not a penny of Foundation funds towards the maintenance of their activities.

The Air Training Corps

If the School was ambivalent towards its responsibilities for out-of-school activities on its premises like allotment tilling and pig keeping, its embracement of the Air Training Corps unit, in contrast, was enthusiastic to a degree. The creation by Royal Warrant of an Air Training Corps, also known as the ATC, under the auspices of the Royal Air Force, in schools and the community nationwide on 5 February 1941[30] excited the patriotic imagination of the Governors, Headmaster, staff and pupils like no other wartime initiative at the School.[31]

By far the longest and most numerous references in the Governors' Minutes and The Lion to any out-of-school activity from 1941 to 1945 were to the School's ATC unit. In September 1941 the ATC was informally inspected by the Governors and in July 1942 was leant the support of the Governors' Welfare Fund following a request for financial assistance. Uniquely, given the fuss they normally kicked up over absence other than for illness or compassionate reasons, the Headmaster and Governors turned a blind eye in

---

30   HM King George VI was its first Air Commodore-in-Chief
31   There was a precedent for a wartime training unit for the armed forces at Hampton Grammar School. Formed in the autumn of 1915, an army cadet unit had proved popular until 1918, after which dwindling enthusiasm amongst pupils had led to its closure in 1921.

1942 and 1943 to the week-long absence during the term of ATC cadets, a group at a time, on visits to RAF stations.[32]

It is unclear as to which of Manders or Crocker was the real driving force during the first few months behind the formation of the ATC. Although Dr Manders was its first commanding officer he quickly disappeared into the forces early in May 1941 and he was succeeded by Flight Officer H Crocker. Harry Crocker's commitment to the School's ATC was without equal and, like Mason, he seems to have had little respect for red tape. But exactly when was the ATC set up at the Grammar School? Crocker was flying by the seat of his pants when, in writing up the formation of an ATC at Hampton in the summer edition of The Lion, he pre-dated the King's Command by stating the unit was *officially established on February 1st ... the day of the formal launching of the ATC throughout the country.'* If there is an inconsistency here, his claim is also difficult to square with his report to the Governors in October 1941, where he simply says 'in February'. Further, the Governors' Meeting of 11 February 1941 had merely *'mooted'* the idea of an ATC, while its formation was not approved until the meeting of 13 May.

What probably happened, though, was that the Headmaster had given his informal consent to its creation at an early date after consulting the Chairman of Governors, given there is no correction of Crocker's statement in the summer edition of The Lion that 'four months of strenuous work' had already been put into getting the School's ATC, Flight 651, off the ground. And there is no doubt that the ATC's popularity nation-wide was mushrooming. Within a year of its inception the number of units had increased from an initial 200 to approximately 1500. This popularity was reflected in the growth in membership of the School's Flight.

The aims of the ATC were unequivocal. Crocker's report to the Governors in October 1941 lays out the rationale of an ATC unit at the School:

'The ATC is an entirely desirable addition to the School's activities. The ATC is the product of an urgent national need. These boys are being trained to safeguard the present or to secure the future ...'

Crocker was a man with a mission. For him, boosting the morale of the young at a time of national crisis was a serious business: even more crucial was their mobilisation in support of the Royal Air Force. Propaganda was a useful tool and Crocker did not shrink from using The Lion and quasi-Churchillian rhetoric to proselytise:

---

32   It is to be wondered whether at times the ATC 'tail' was wagging the Grammar School 'dog'. See later

97

'A word now to cadets. The ATC has been called the younger brother of the Royal Air Force and boys who join it are setting foot on the high road to that magnificent fighting service. It is a hard road, to be entered upon only by those whose one ambition it is to be fit mentally and physically for service with the RAF. The road will call for grit and courage and abundant effort, and for a new sense of values in which the word "give" ousts the word "take". The road must be kept full of boys travelling on, as the need is urgent and imperative. And the road must be taken with pride. We, as individuals and as a Unit, must be openly and avowedly proud of our association with men whose standards have never been surpassed in history, and we must show that pride by diligent seeking of those high standards in our own persons and conduct. Give to the ATC through your own Unit the best that is in you, at all times and in all places. Face squarely and courageously the responsibilities that are now yours, and you will meet all the graver responsibilities that lie ahead.'

The incongruity of his exhortation becomes obvious when set against his statement in the same article, that he and his predecessor, Dr Manders, were in agreement that the ATC was a new form of war effort and that no-one in the country knew how to run an ATC unit. Although the ATC would be at a stage of experimentation for more than a year, Crocker continued to romanticise the importance of the ATC by describing it in October 1941 as a *'national institution'*, a claim difficult to square with the collapse of its predecessor, the Air Defence Cadet Force, within a year of its inception in 1938.

Crocker, of course, had no control over which boys were permitted to join the ATC and which were not. This 'national institution' could not, for instance, include German or Austrian Jewish refugee Hamptonians like David Franklin or George Kerpner, who had been defined by the War Office as 'aliens.' However, the ATC unit took the bold step of admitting the two boys, hoping perhaps that higher authority would not step in and eject them. Certainly, the Headmaster's earlier joust with the Home Office on Franklin's behalf, as we have already seen, demonstrated his sentiment – and that of his staff – concerning the boys' loyalty. However, both boys were dismissed from the ATC, on the instructions of the Air Ministry, a few months after they joined in 1941. Kerpner reflects on the poignant circumstances of his dismissal from the ATC. His bout against Les Woollett, a local champion, in the unit's boxing tournament, had been imminent:

'A telegram arrived from the Air Ministry informing the squadron that it apparently harboured an enemy alien in their midst. It demanded the prompt removal of the offending person named, which was me. I found it a little perverse that, as a declared enemy of the German nation, I had had to flee the country for

dear life, whilst now, as an enemy alien here, I was considered to threaten this country's security. My pain was lessened by the thought that I would not now have to fight Les Woollett. Be that as it may, my career in the ATC was finished, but I probably had the kindest dishonourable discharge ever given to any recruit. Though he did not have any tears in his eyes, Mr Crocker, our severe commander, could not quite suppress a smile of sympathy as he dismissed me, saluting smartly as ever.'[33]

Harry Crocker may not have been the most plausible of publicists, but he and his officer colleagues, Frank Steffens, 'Sid' Barton and, later, JJB Wolfe, were highly effective administrators of the ATC. Even though they were recruiting 15 year olds whose imaginations were already fired up by recent experiences and memories, positive or negative, of the Battle of Britain and the Blitz, their success was almost total in that nearly all of the older Hamptonians till 1945 were at some stage volunteers in the ATC. By October 1941, the ATC comprised 50 recruits and a number of older former pupils who were permitted to join in preparation for entry into the RAF on call-up. In his report Crocker described the ATC curriculum: drill, PT, maths, navigation, aircraft recognition, signals, and the workings of an 'internal combustion engine'. Considerable emphasis was placed on drill routines and games, with regular football fixtures against other local ATC units. Crocker reported that a visit to Hurricane assembly shops had taken place and some flying from the airfield there was observed. (The location of the RAF station is blanked out in the report. Not even the confidentiality of a Governors' Meeting could be trusted!). The first national ATC camp (at RAF Halton) was held during the summer holiday of 1941, attended by 700 boys. The Hampton Grammar contingent included 23 Kingston boys and was awarded Best on Parade, with Flight Sergeant Rudkin singled out as outstanding in ability and promise.

All this was heady stuff to 'RAF-struck' adolescent recruits. An antiquated de-commissioned Tiger Moth was parked in one of the fives courts for ground tuition purposes. Even 'drill' could be exciting – John Claxton found satisfaction in his squad's meticulous execution from memory of marching movements without orders – while the unfortunate George Kerpner was exhilarated by his discovery of the star Betelgeuse in his all too brief membership of the air navigation classes. Pat Gubbins, a working-boy member of the ATC whose fortunes we followed during 1940, says in his reminiscences that while the ATC was useful as a means of keeping touch with his old friends and the school, he

---

33   George Kerpner continued to fire-watch at the School, arguably as undesirable a front-line activity for a
     listed 'alien' as membership of the ATC.

Hampton School ATC, September 1941 (*picture in 'School by the Thames', page 52*)

quickly realised that it was '*a serious business*'. He attended his first ATC meeting on 13 May 1941. The first thing he did was some drill. After passing a medical, which included a colour-blindness test, he attended on Mondays and Thursdays after work. What he learned from his schoolmaster and civilian instructors about navigation, meteorology, signalling in Morse code with an Aldis lamp, as well as parade ground drills, stood him in good stead later for his service with the RAF. There was a lighter side too. He played football for the ATC each Saturday afternoon and was one of the few who managed to get a 'flip' in a Wellington bomber. In February 1943, he and two others from the Hampton ATC joined the RAF, having successfully negotiated an RAF selection board at Euston. All three were selected for training as either pilots, navigators or bomb aimers.

The carrot for any cadet was to go on a week-long visit to an RAF station, preferably during term-time. Flight Sergeant 'Bo' Bowyer, aged 16½, wrote in the school magazine of his six-strong party's experience at 'Muddlecombe', his pseudonym for the RAF station somewhere in East Suffolk. Their fun was endless: sessions on Link trainers (ground flight simulators), flights in Tiger Moths, crawling over Whitley, Manchester and Wellington bombers, conversations with fighter pilots in the crew room about flying Spitfires, looking over a Hampden bomber that had just arrived badly damaged from an operation, cleaning the twin Browning machine guns off a Lysander and clay pigeon shooting for a prize of forbidden fruits – 20 Canadian cigarettes. And the senior NCO's experience would not be complete before he was brought down to earth on his final flight. The pilot put the Tiger Moth into bumpy turbulence that caused 'Bo' Bowyer to throw up his fish and chips lunch, which, he said, '... *gave the others plenty to do until dinner, cleaning up the mess I had made. They say that everyone is sick one day ...*'

The ATC, accorded Squadron status in 1942, went from strength to strength for the rest of the war. Activities after school during the winter had been made possible at an early stage by the Air Ministry's funding of blackout materials. Numbers of ATC members reached 120 at one point in 1943, due to an Air Ministry decision to lower the ATC age recruitment point from 16 to 15.3 and the slowness of the RAF in absorbing the large numbers of service-age young men waiting to join the RAF. With Bomber Command casualties alone exceeding 12,000 killed or missing between 1942 and 1943 – the sort of information certainly not available to the public at the time, let alone to Hampton schoolboys – the log jam eased through 1944 and into 1945. Proficiency Tests in subjects like navigation, signalling and aircraft recognition had been introduced at an early stage, for which a pass-rate in excess of 90% was continually achieved by the unit. In sum, membership of the ATC required an enormous commitment by both staff and boys, but, as Michael Brudenell infers, it ate into student study time.

ATC cadets and Whitley bomber
(Imperial War Museum)

The Headmaster was proud of the ATC. It fitted in with a military man's wartime scheme of things – commitment, discipline, service and self-sacrifice. He was especially conscious of the implications of self-sacrifice. Only a perusal of the wartime editions of The Lion and his extensive 'Notes from the Headmaster's Desk', as well as of his papers in the Imperial War Museum, can bring home to a reader the depth of his feelings for 'his' Old Boys who were on active service. His summary of the work of the ATC, in his 'Russia Account' in June 1945, is both brief and factual. The introductory sentences say everything about Flight 651's achievement by 1945:

'The Air Training Corps is a national institution, born in February 1941 and likely, so far as now can be foreseen, to continue after the Japanese War. This school raised a Flight (later a squadron) from the outset and the School Squadron is reckoned to be one of the best in the country not only as to examination work, but as to formal drill and skill at games ...'

The Scout Troop

In contrast to the ATC, the Second Hampton (Grammar School) Boy Scout troop was, historically, very much part of a 'national movement' from before the Great War. However, immediately war broke out in September 1939, all scout troops, and not least the Grammar School's, were hit by the call-up of its scoutmasters. The School troop was quickly reduced to one master, HS 'Bull' Moodey: he, however, left in 1941 to take up a headmastership in the Midlands. To add to the difficulties, not all scouting members of the School were members of the School's troop. John Claxton, for instance, was a member of the Sunbury troop where Michael Brudenell was troop leader, while Mike Tadman was a member of the Sea Scouts in Hampton Hill. Had it not been for the presence and important work of a local Old Hamptonian scoutmaster, Ron Pyne, and able senior scouters like Robin Catford and Alan Meacock, the School troop would have collapsed. As it was, as Mason recorded in his 'Russia Account', numbers of between 50 and 60 were maintained to the end of the war. This popularity was to be found chiefly at the 11 to 14 year old level: the membership of 15 year olds was severely affected from 1941 by competition from the ATC. Ron Pyne resented losing his scouts to the ATC and made it quite clear to one young Hamptonian, Jack Wells, that dual membership was impossible. Although there was no legal impediment to dual membership, weekend commitments clashed. Crocker could not have endeared himself to Pyne by forming an 'unofficial junior' ATC group which boys could join in the year they turned 15. For Wells it was no contest. An avid aircraft spotter who cycled round the local airstrips to 'collect' unusual RAF aircraft sightings, he left the Troop to join the ATC.

Was this an indication that the Boy Scouts had become out-of-date, a movement that had sprung out of bushcraft and a war fought forty years ago in South Africa? Not really, for within the first few days of the declaration of war in September 1939, some boy scouts were 'mobilised' by telegram from Imperial Headquarters (of the scouting movement) to ' ... report for urgent duty at Imperial Headquarters'.[34] As we noticed earlier, their duties were, for instance, to act as messengers. Scout troops up and down the country filled sandbags, assisted the elderly or, as John Claxton did in Sunbury, pushed the two-wheeler scout cart around collecting cardboard and soft wood for a local factory. Then there was the erection of Morrison air-raid shelters in the homes of those who were less physically capable. The Second Hampton (Grammar School) Boy Scouts put up more than twenty shelters later in 1941. Mike Tadman recalls the efforts of his Sea Scouts troop in Hampton Hill.

'The Morrison [shelter] ... was a sheet steel structure, the size and shape of a dining table which would accommodate three or four people ... and was calculated to bear the weight of a house collapsing on to it ... It was a pretty massive affair, delivered in "flat pack" form, and assembling it was an evening's work for half-a-dozen young lads. This was where the Scouts came in. We visited people's

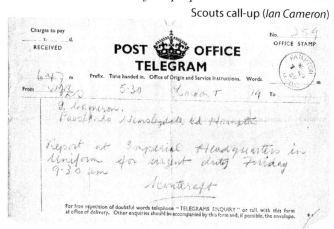

Scouts call-up (Ian Cameron)

---

34   Telegram, 7-9-39: Imperial Scouting HQ to Ian Cameron (OH), School Archive

Wood Pigeon patrol 1942
(Alan Meacock)

AA Meacock   JCL Clarke
JD Wells   PA Glenister
HJ Lee   NE Clarke   ML Catford

houses by arrangement and erected their shelters for them. They sometimes tried to tip us, but of course we couldn't accept. A cup of tea and a piece of cake was as far as we would go.[35]

Outdoor camps were a great attraction, although these were available as well, with differences in emphasis, in the ATC and, of course, the School's summer harvest outings. Pre-war, the School troop would go down to Cornwall or the Scilly Isles. After 1939 the school field or Broadstone Warren, south of East Grinstead, had to suffice. Still, it was a great adventure for a 12 year old like Jack Wells to put a large rucksack on his back, and – 'watched in fear and trepidation by his mother'– set off on his bicycle to the Broadstone camp more than 30 miles away. There, without much adult supervision, he would practise his bushcraft and skills for his badges and, in short, have a jolly good time away from it all. John Claxton was a member of a troop near home, the First Sunbury. He enjoyed working for his first class badges. The last one was to be earned by cycling 30 miles, setting up camp, making a fire and cooking one's own food. However, he and his friends decided to take a fatal short cut on the final, crucial task:

'When we got to the camp-site, the girl guides were camping nearby and they kindly cooked our food. I thought we were pretty resourceful, but the scoutmaster found out (his wife was the guide-mistress) and he failed us.'

In sum, the key difference between the Scouts and the ATC, in a wartime context, was that the former was adjunct to the Home Front, performing the social role of assistance to the community, whereas the ATC was an RAF recruitment ground, offering specific preparation to young volunteers for future service in the Air Force.

---

35   The Morrison shelter saved countless lives, not least those of John Lovesey and his youngest brother in 1944

Harvest Camps

The School's wartime summer holiday harvest camps were, like the ATC and the scouts, a collective contribution to the war effort and beloved by all. Camps were memorable for different reasons.

Michael Brudenell has already recounted, for instance, how the first camp, billed as a forestry camp, near Aldershot in 1940 was disrupted from time to time by the Luftwaffe. For the Headmaster, the harvest camp at Cholsey in 1941 was a great success. His report to the Governors told of a party of 33 boys, a master and an Old Hamptonian helping local farmers with the harvest. While three boys worked in the kitchen the others spent a total of '*5482 hours*' working in the fields, for which they were '*well paid*' by '*reasonable*' farmers. The Berkshire War Agricultural Committee arranged the use of the village school for 'living quarters' and obtained blankets and palliasses. The Local Womens' Voluntary Service loaned out stoves and cooked the main meal of the day. The local residents were very kind and the local Headmaster very helpful. There were no accidents, he said, but two boys developed severe skin conditions from the bites of harvest bugs. Casualties negligible therefore and, clearly, the regiment had done well.

Peter Hodges remembered the 1942 Cholsey camp and Mr Bitmead's farm for his first taste of alcohol. At the end of their stay he and his four companions were paid their wages (at 2d an hour) and then directed to the farmhouse. There the farmer sat them down and gave them home-brewed beer which, Hodges says, made them '*giggly*'. There were fun and games at the 1945 Compton camp in Berkshire. Bailing straw on a combine harvester was the serious part. John Claxton remembers what he and three others from his form at school got up to elsewhere:

Harvest Camp
(Ron Keevil)

'On one occasion we were given a box of matches and told to burn the stubble in a field. There was no supervision. We certainly burned the stubble and nearly took a row of cottages with it! Another day we were put on weeding mangelwurzels. They were in rows in a huge field which seemed a mile long. It was so boring that for a change we weeded out all the mangels in one row and left in the weeds. One of the masters [Jammy James] at that camp was keen on ballroom dancing and we had dancing lessons twice a week in the village hall, with the girls from the village. Naturally the village boys were jealous and there were fights.'

Out of hours

Outdoor activities were by no means confined to participating in organised pursuits. As we observed earlier, there were individual enthusiasms, like skating on iced-up Bushy Park ponds in the depths of winter and swimming in the Thames between Sunbury and the Bell Inn, Hampton, in summer. As well as a keen swimmer, Alan Duddy was an outdoor lad who enjoyed fishing and hunting rabbits in and around the reservoirs between Hatherop Park, Kempton Park and Hanworth. The large reservoir that stretched up to the pumping station in Hanworth could be accessed from behind Hatherop Park, for instance. He and friends would climb over the fence onto the reservoir bank and fish for roach and perch, all the time keeping a look out for the arrival of the water bailiffs, at which point, he says, *'we scarpered!'*. More unusual were the rabbiting expeditions he conducted with a friend, an awkward giant of a lad (*'about 6'7"'*), who attended Rectory School. Duddy recalls:

'He would bring his father's sawn off shotgun which he would tuck down the front of his trousers. I don't know where his father got the cartridges from and it wasn't very accurate. I would bring my dog, a golden spaniel, and we would hunt rabbits around the reservoirs. My poor old dog went blind in the end because of going into the brambles.'

We have already recorded Derek Fisher's gratitude to the GIs of Bushy Park over a flying bomb incident. He and his friends had a different reason to be grateful to their local GIs.

'*The Americans and the many girls attracted to the camp were of course a matter of great curiosity for us lads. A good evening out was for us to cycle in a group along the river tow path near Kingston with torches shining them on the couples in the long grass. Our extra school education developed by leaps and bounds at that time!*'

If, for Fisher and his friends, 'the university of life' had its beginnings along the Thames tow path, Jammy James' dance lessons, young mistresses, late war parties in Manor Gardens and romantic trysts in Carlisle Park were the catalysts of adolescent awakening for others. On one harvest camp a Hamptonian fraternised so closely with the local girls that he was sent home. One 16 year old, however, seemed to lead a life from 1941 that would have beggared the belief of his contemporaries had they known. More than sixty years later, David Franklin describes his adolescent sexual status before turning 16:

'*I was a virgin until the time I should have been sowing my oats with the girls at the school next door but when you are shy and five foot four and have no English, it gets a bit difficult. Around the time I was fifteen I had a great crush on a dark haired beautie called Katie next door at Lady Eleanor Holles but that ebbed away when she married ... one of my classmates, but I never even dared tell him about it.*'

Having commenced the last eighteen months of his General School Certificate studies at the School Franklin seemed to embark upon a double life. On the one hand, while his classmates were embroiled in games – David wasn't a games player – or in the ATC – David was a listed 'enemy alien' – he was doing his homework for his matric, going to the cinema, hanging out with Michael Brudenell, listening to jazz records with another school friend, Brian Biles, and helping his parents with their clothing business in Soho. On the other hand, Franklin says, he was losing his virginity with the help of 'Grace Thompson', his father's 'secretary' at a flat in Chelsea owned by 'Uncle' Charles, an old family friend from Berlin days. David Franklin's escapades, aided and abetted by raffish adult confidants in the seedy world of the 'Chelsea Closets' and Soho pubs, as revealed in his racy autobiography, cannot be corroborated. However, they have a context in the amorality of life after dark in a demi-monde wartime West End, discussed in other histories of the period.[36]

For many Hamptonians, the most popular activity, as we have seen, was scouting. Indeed, a 'Public Opinion Poll', conducted at the School by a group calling themselves

36   David Franklin: 'Dave's Tales'; Book Guild Press, 2008. For further reading see, for instance, Juliet Gardiner's 'Over Here: the GIs in wartime Britain'; Collins & Brown 1992, and Stuart Hylton's 'Their Darkest Hour, the hidden history of the Home Front'; Sutton 2001

the Bureau of Public Opinion and published in The Lion,[37] found that 49% of those canvassed were members of scout troops, and were predominantly younger boys.

Individual accounts place 'picture', or 'cinema' going as a frequently enjoyed entertainment. Yet according to the 'Opinion Poll', only 4% of the sample said they visited cinema once a week – there were a number of cinemas in the Borough and in Richmond – and 27% once a fortnight. The Blitz did not deter a keen picture-goer like Peter Hornsby. On Saturday 26 October, he set off for the 'Premier' Cinema at the top of the road from Richmond Bridge during the fourth air raid that day. His diary records:

'... The All Clear went [at 1.50 pm] as I got to the Premier to see "Turnabout", with John Hubbard, Carole Landis, Adolphe Menjou, and 'Gentlemen of Venture', with Wilfrid Lawson and Norah Swinburne. Both good films, specially the latter. Probably better than both was 'Britain Can Take It', an M of I [Ministry of Information] film showing air raids on London and how Britons take it – a commentary by Quentin Reynolds (American war reporter). While I was there, quite a few raids, at 1.52 till 2.9. Raid 6 2.12 to 2.44. Raid 7 at 3.19 to 3.40. Raid 8 at 4.3 till 4.30 ...'

A hobby unique to the period of the Blitz was, as John Lovesey mentioned earlier, the collection of air raid souvenirs. Mike Tadman describes them:

'The most common were anti-aircraft shell splinters, alarming pieces of jagged steel two or three inches long, and pieces of the driving band ... that girdled the shell ... I had quite a collection of these bits and pieces, as did all my friends, but I never could come by the most coveted souvenir of all, the fins of an incendiary bomb. The Germans dropped these in huge quantities. They were cylindrical, about sixteen inches long and perhaps three inches in diameter, and made of solid magnesium, with green-painted sheet metal fins riveted to one end. They were dropped in clusters, and wherever they hit they detonated and burned with an intense flame, until they were consumed completely, except for the fins. When they dropped in open ground, you found a little pile of grey ash with the fins close by.'

At home, the most essential pastime was listening to the BBC. In 1944, according, once again, to the 'Public Opinion Poll', Hamptonians' most popular wireless programmes were Monday at Eight, ITMA, The Brains Trust, Happidrome and Music Hall, a mixture of serious and light entertainment. The boosting of morale in wartime was axiomatic. Like so many of his contemporaries Mike Tadman remembers numerous comedy programmes, some of them classics like ITMA, with the famous 'It's That Man Again' Tommy Handley, music-hall transmissions and concerts. 'At 5 o'clock every evening we had the Children's Hour, which put on some very

---

37   The Bureau was nicknamed 'Gestapo Work'

good plays and general interest programmes. I remember one playwright, L. du Garde Peach, who wrote very good historical plays for children, which were both educational and entertaining.'

Unsurprisingly, the core of listening to the 'wireless', a more commonly used term than 'the radio', was to BBC news. At 9 o'clock each evening the chimes of Big Ben introduced the news and households fell silent. Newsreaders became famous, like John Snagge who announced the fall of France and the D-Day landings. Wartime media news was not always what it seemed, though. Derek Fisher offers a retrospective comparison of the dissemination of news, between the BBC and newspapers:

'We listened to the news a lot. We believed everything we heard and we thought the word propaganda meant lies being put out by the enemy. The same with the newspapers – I remember a placard heading for the Evening News on the crucial day of the Battle Britain, 150 ALL OUT alluding to the figure of German losses as if it were a cricket score. I believe the true number was around half of this figure.'

Boyhood reading matter veered from the sublime to the gorblimey. At Hampton Grammar, boys were given every encouragement to read, as Tadman relates:

'We were all avid readers. In English we were given a set book every term, which we had to work through. I remember in the second form, there was one book we all especially coveted – Adventures in the Rifle Brigade, a memoir of the Peninsula War by Captain Kincaid. When 'Doughnut' [Harrison] announced that this was to be our book for the next term, the whole form actually cheered.'

Many boys adored Richmal Crompton's Billy Bunter books which, like comics, were abhorred by their teachers. Fourth-former Pat Gubbins kept a comprehensive list of his reading habit in 1940: his favourite author was PG Wodehouse, Agatha Christie received a mixture of 'goods' and 'poors', and Edgar Wallace received the thumbs up for 'The Gaunt Stranger'. The most extraordinary volume on his list was 'Mein Kamf' [sic] by Adolf Hitler, for which his remark was 'Good'.[38] If, however, a pupil plagiarised his reading in the pursuit of literary excellence, he was quickly rumbled. The 10 year old John Lovesey attempted to impress his new English teacher, Mr Bentham, using the plot from one of Rafael Sabatini's sea yarns he had been reading, to compose an imaginary piece about pirates. Back came his work, with the top mark and a salutary reminder, 'Reminiscences of Rafael Sabatini at his best: don't do it again.'

At the other end of the spectrum were comics. The most popular were the Wizard, the Rover, the Champion and the Hotspur. Published weekly, these had a

---

38   Gubbins revealed in a conversation with this author in 2008 that he borrowed 'Mein Kampf' from the public library

cover containing a garish illustration of one of the stories inside, and within, page after page of close-set type. Story lines were a mixture of remarkable blood-lust, particularly towards the enemy, and the wildly improbable. One favourite story was about Wilson the Wonder Athlete, born in 1795 and still going strong in 1938 when he ran a 3-minute mile. Many contemporaries remember they couldn't have enough of them, buying one title, reading it and then, at school, swopping it for one of the others.

Making Do

The bottom line of home life in those times, despite the destructive awfulness of war that could suddenly visit families, was to make do and get on with life. It wasn't easy. Privations at home included the sharing of bathwater: only five inches of bathwater was allowed per family once a week. One toilet roll was allowed per family per week. Coal was almost non-existent and only one gas ring for cooking dinner was permitted.

Parents bore the brunt of difficulties. Mothers queued endlessly for food and other necessities. If anyone complained about service, they encountered bad-temperedness and the snappy response that became a cliché, 'Don't you know there's a war on?' Shortages increased as the war worsened. Rationing became more severe – cheese, eggs, jam and clothing soon on the list with butter, cream, tea, sugar, meat and petrol . John Claxton remembers the issue of ration books, partly for portions of specific food, such as butter (2 oz a week) and partly for a chance of less basic items, (for instance tinned food), by the use of a points system. The only eggs officially available were dried eggs in powder form. Yet, says Claxton, 'I never remember not having enough to eat', a view echoed by other Hamptonian contemporaries.

'Making do' might require tactical flexibility with resources. A bartering arrangement enabled families to get round rationing. Claxton's family took no sugar in their tea and their surplus sugar could always be exchanged with other people for other rationed food – 'this was the fringe of the so-called black market', says Claxton. When business was slack David Franklin's family, who were clothing manufacturers, exchanged surplus cloth-purchasing coupons

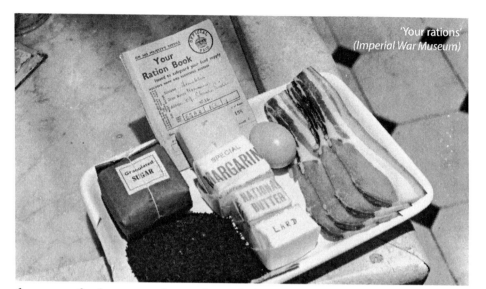

for meat, fresh eggs and petrol. And then some people were favoured by shopkeepers, hence the term 'under-the-counter'. Luxuries, remembers Mike Tadman, were scarce:

'Sweet rationing came in; two ounces (e.g. one small bar of chocolate) a week. That was when you could get it! Just because a ration was prescribed, there was no guarantee that it would be available. Oranges and orange juice were reserved for toddlers, issued only on children's ration books, and bananas simply disappeared. As was pointed out at the time, by the end of the war there were children of six or seven years old who had actually never seen a banana. As far as we children were concerned, it was at Christmas that the privations became most noticeable. Of course toys were short. There was no production capacity to spare for fripperies such as decorations, and the black-out precluded any outdoor lights. Turkeys were a rarity, and most people settled for a chicken, which was considered a delicacy anyway.'

If, however, a boy was lucky enough, as Dennis Barnes was, he could spend school holidays on a farm. A family friend farmed near Wendover where, Dennis remembers, '... *during those days of rationing, unlimited servings of eggs and bacon were a true delight.'*

Once home finances were stretched to breaking point, might a boy's place at the School be jeopardised because of the onerousness of fees? The minutes of Governors' meetings record that a number of parents each year applied successfully to the Governors for fee remission. Derek Fisher's mother had to go up to the School at one point to ask if the school fee (£5 guineas

(TSO)

a term) could be reduced because her husband was ill and business was bad. It was reduced to £2 guineas. The proportion of fee reduction to the total number of applicants, though, is not known.

School 'extras' could be an additional burden. The School's new dining facility, however, was a blessing to a majority of parents, as we have already seen. But what about that necessity, the school uniform? What if – recorded the minutes of a Governors' meeting in February 1942 – the Board of Education wanted schools to withdraw or reduce to a minimum any requirements hitherto imposed on pupils for a *special outfit distinctive of the particular school*'? On the one hand, the School Rule Book of 1942 took no notice of this. The school uniform requirement was the school cap (4/1d each) and '*... the general school blazer [which] is of plain black cloth with gilt buttons and without edging. The School blazer badge in house - colours may be worn on this type only.*' In practice, however, Mason was already turning a blind eye. While the wearing of caps continued, blazers, as Mike Tadman remembers, '*... were not strictly compulsory, and when clothes rationing was introduced later in the War, any sort of dress code went out of the window. Some of us were literally "out-at-elbows".*' In July 1943, the Governors and Headmaster, in effect, amended the Rules concerning '*house shoes*', ordaining that pupils would be required to wear

Pat Gubbins' pocket money
(*Charles Letts Ltd* and *Pat Gubbins*)

house shoes or go in stockinged or bare feet, 'notwithstanding being bare-footed on wooden floors in winter'.

The availability of pocket money for Hamptonians seemed to vary considerably. On the one hand, in a brief survey of '40%' of the School, conducted in the 'Bureau of Public Opinion's Poll', 40% of the sample said they received 3/- a week while 10% said they could ask for as much money as they pleased. A different picture emerges from Pat Gubbins' diary. A detailed record of his personal income and expenditure for March 1940 – when he was on school holidays for a fortnight – shows no discernible pocket money grant from his family, compared with February when his elder brother, Jack, who was in employment in the City gave him a shilling. Other than an Easter present of 1/6d from his mother, his only income was 6/- from four days odd jobbing for 'Jammy' James at Denmead School during the holidays. Visits to 'the pictures' cost him 4/7d, while his expenditure on sweets was 10d.[39]

---

[39] Boys were actively discouraged by the School from taking employment of any kind during term time

Those who Struggled

For some of its wartime pupils, Hampton Grammar was an academic struggle. Although no evidence survives in the School's records as to why individual boys came to grief, the main pressure was clear. Once the School was fully assembled in January 1940, and in spite of severe staffing difficulties, Mason seemed intent on maintaining academic standards, full stop. While the Governors, for their part, were compassionate throughout towards families in difficulties over the fees, there is little discernible evidence of concessions on academic matters till 1942.

Reservations have already been expressed about the stance being taken by the Headmaster and Governors on academic matters when, in February 1940, they threatened two boys in their General School Certificate year[40] with exclusion for poor work. A year later, the Blitz not yet over, with staff continuing to come and go, the Headmaster and Governors again expressed their disquiet concerning the 'unsatisfactory' 1940 autumn term reports of five – unnamed – boys. Moreover, warning letters had been sent to the parents that their sons' places would be withdrawn unless subsequent reports showed a marked improvement. It was said, in all cases, their reports had been unsatisfactory for some time. It was not stated whether 'unsatisfactory' meant in effort or in achievement.

Set these threats against Hampton Grammar's public examination results in the summer of 1940 and it is clear where Mason and his Governors were coming from. In October 1940, the Headmaster reported a larger number of failures than usual 'in the general'. The 1941 GSC[41] results were worse, Mason reporting a record number of failures, 22 out of the 81 who sat. However, there were no further threats of disciplinary action from the Governing Body until July 1942 when it was noted that an increased number – eleven – of unsatisfactory reports had been brought to Governors' attention, although no warning letters were sent in consequence. It is not clear why the Governors had gone so quiet on matters of academic discipline, yet a clue may lie in the comment by Mason on the 1941 results. '*The 2 streamed forms did well as usual, the others did very badly and suffered most from constant staff changes.*' Three conclusions can be drawn from this: first, that the weaker examination forms were stuck with weaker teaching; second, that

---

40 Both survived to the end of the summer term and therefore almost certainly sat their public examinations
41 General School Certificate (GSC) = modern GCSE; 'Highers' = modern A Levels

the problem of endemic staff change was affecting most of the pupils; and third, that the Governors seemed no longer prepared to discipline pupils in the light of Mason's reservation.

The Governors' apparent reluctance to discipline pupils, however, makes the events of the summer of 1942 incomprehensible. Within a fortnight of the submission of eleven unsatisfactory end of year reports, the Governors had required five pupils – names, ages and forms unspecified – to leave at the end of the term because of unsatisfactory reports. No extraordinary meeting had been called to decide on the matter, no warning letters had been issued during the past eighteen months that might have precipitated the exclusions and there is no evidence to suggest that the five excluded numbered amongst the eleven stated earlier at the meeting in July. It was not until the Governors met three months later that the exclusions were recorded, without comment.

This was an unsatisfactory state of affairs and pupils were the casualties. Mercifully, for other strugglers, the School's approach to academic standards softened from 1943. Ironically, from a significant improvement in public examination results that summer, there was a decline in the GSC pass-rate over the next two years. Only one set of unsatisfactory school reports – nine in total – was presented to the Governors for review before the end of the war and that was in February 1943. Action was neither threatened nor taken. This did not mean that problems concerning public examinations henceforth were ignored. The Headmaster described the 1943 results as 'less good than usual, due to the accumulated effect of the Blitz, shelter-dodging and frequent changes of staff'. In July 1944, having reported that the public exams could not have been taken under worse conditions, Mason evaluated the GSC exam cohort as consisting of two good exam forms and two bad forms. Three months later he was to confirm his prediction. Despite a leap in the numbers taking GSC, he reported that 'the results were poor for a school of this size, but this was expected due to war-time circumstances'. He may even have under-stated the effects of the flying bomb menace, which could see frightened examinees scurrying suddenly under their desks. Even the eleven Highers candidates – Hampton's academic cream – suffered the greatest number of failures since 1940. While the 1945 examinations, sat after VE Day, produced the best set of GSC and Highers results since 1939, this evoked a curious reflection from Mason in his report to the Governors in October 1945. In his opinion, ' ... the two bad forms were the victims of war time circumstances here and at home', and he regarded the 'very bad form' as one averaging only 42.4% per examination script, the one that had done 'extremely well' averaging 58.6%.

'Slackers' Parade'

Mason's obsession with academic results as Headmaster seemed to be underpinned in part by a basic assumption that academic failure was the result of pupil laziness. In practice this assumption was inherent in the disciplinary system he had created for 'slackers' before the war, described in his article for The Lion a few years after his retirement. While what he put in place in the 1920s underwent a shift in emphasis during the war, as we have seen, he does reflect on the effect it may have had on pupils.

Even the title of Mason's article, and the first sentence, suggest the possibility of a hidden menace: fear.

"Please Duplicate"
Does the heading send a cold shiver of apprehension down the OH reader's back?'

For a boy to be told at the end of term to make a copy of his report, which had been deemed unsatisfactory and bore the stamp, *'Please Duplicate'*, was to put him on the road to perdition, even though this academic Via Dolorosa had its well-defined and attainable exits. Mason and his Second Master were formidable figures of authority and one or the other interviewed the *'Slackers' Parade'*, starting on the first Wednesday of the new term. If the *'slacker's'* subsequent fortnightly grade cards did not improve, as a *'hardened sinner'* he was punished with the cane. An indirect punishment was that by having to report to the 'Slacker's Parade', the boy was also deprived of his games afternoon. What amounted to a fear of deprivation, Mason believes that this had often been *'a wonderfully effective'* punishment before the war, but since 1939, *'the remarkable change that ... seems to have overcome the schoolboy's attitude to team games of football and cricket has now ruled out this particular form of stimulus'*. Given the degree of disruption caused by the war, this decline of enthusiasm cannot have surprised Mason, even though it ran contrary to his adherence to the team spirit. Fear of the cane seemed to be an insufficient deterrent to a small minority: Mason refers to, '... the depressing task of administering C.P. [corporal punishment] to the tail end (both senses)[42] of the parade.'

We already know about what happened to the handful of boys who, after three or four terms of unsatisfactory reports, had their cases put before the Governors. Apart from the inference we can make that certain of these young academic recidivists may have been beaten several times a term for a whole year, Mason confirms that after a warning had been issued to the parents, a boy's place at the School was on the line: *'In very bad cases the Governors asked that they should take the boy away, and in the days when that was possible*[43] *they insisted on that being done'.*

Mason certainly had pangs of conscience about the system. While recalling the pleasure of congratulating those who had improved and were taken off the list, he said he had found, *'… a deeper interest in the interviews with the hardened sinners, in the attempt to get under their skins and discover what was wrong. There was always the almost terrifying thought that it was hard to distinguish between the slow and the lazy …'.* Mason asks: *'Was the 'slacker' misunderstood? He probably was in many cases. Were his home conditions against him? Often they were. In the records there are … [homes where] … education as the grammar school of today knows, was little appreciated, or, in some cases, that in poverty decent homework was impossible … A few slackers were probably not fit physically. I can think of five who developed T.B. [tuberculosis] very soon … I can think of at least three Hamptonians to whom I must have seemed both brutal and unjust. Whatever they felt at the time, however, they have long since forgiven me. One is dead and the other two are as loyal OHs as could be found.'*

And there lies the rub. Notwithstanding Mason's reservations – and these he may have had by 1943 - his verdict on the system was vindicatory. He spends much of the article listing the numerous later successes among his *'slackers'*, explaining that the system did them more good than harm, that the weekly 'parades' enabled him to get to know 'many hundreds' of pupils he would otherwise have known 'very superficially'. And among them, he says, *'… are many of my best OH friends today'.* No mention is made, though, of the paramount importance of the School's examination results that we examined earlier, no admission that incompetent or fragmented teaching might have been a contributory cause of pupil travail.

---

43   The 1944 Education Act deprived the Governors of the absolute right of expulsion

'A Grammar School Failure?'

While Mason sheds some light on why pupils may have 'failed' at the Grammar School, this author's researches has yielded only one pupil-source that suggests the nature of academic 'failure' at Hampton during the war. Although the pupil's time at the School overruns our period by two years the circumstances of his experiences may well have been little different had he arrived earlier. Dennis Barnes (OH 1944-1947) reminisced in two letters to the author in 2008. He titled his memories, *A Grammar School Failure?'*

Dennis Barnes arrived at Hampton from Chatsworth School, Hounslow, on a scholarship in 1944. The transition was not easy. His parents had separated in 1936. His mother was at work all day, his elder sister and brother together at another senior school in Hounslow. Whereas home was only a ten minute walk from Chatsworth, and it had been possible to get home for lunch, Hampton Grammar was over an hour away, on the 33 bus as far as Twickenham station and then the 667 trolley bus to Hampton.

In retrospect, Barnes thinks his main problem was to do with regimentation:

'Chatsworth junior school had been fairly easy going. Possibly because of the war, the numbers were small and the staff mostly older females. The Grammar was stricter. Outdoor shoes not allowed past the cloakroom. The school moved between each lesson, in single file on the left. School was a six day week. Wednesday afternoon was organised sport. To compensate, lessons were held on Saturday mornings, while on Saturday afternoon it was expected that pupils would participate, of their own volition, in team sports.'

Even so, he didn't mind homework – traditionally, a tough nut to crack for new boys – and he enjoyed other activities that, '... *kept mind and body in trim, like the buying and selling of comic books, playing miniature cricket in the gym entrance ways and "bung the barrel" in the fives courts until it was banned.'*

Things went wrong, though. *'Unfortunately, for one reason or another, I became bored with all the travelling and lessons and decided that I could find better things to do with my time.'* So Dennis played truant: so much so that before he realized it, most of the school year had passed. Just when the School picked up on his unauthorised absences is unclear. However, says Dennis, *'Mother and I were "invited" to meet with 'Bossy' Mason to discuss my future. It was agreed, that since I was not stupid, I should be given the chance to repeat the first year.'*

So there Dennis was, the following September, back in Form 1A. This time he resolved to make a go of it. He was accepted by his peers and elected Vice Form Captain.

'I found life much easier and managed to achieve a number of 'A's and 'B's on the report cards. During this year I played cricket for the form. I was a fair bowler and, in one particular game, my captain scored a century and I did the hat trick. This feat was reported at the following Monday morning's assembly. Billy Horne, the Captain, and I were selected to play in a First Form Team to play against a local junior school [Denmead]. Mr James was headmaster at that school. On arrival at the venue one Saturday, both teams were in all white, with the exception of yours truly. I had a white shirt, but had not been able to get white pants. I wore grey. It was decided that this was not 'good form' and that I should be relegated to Twelfth Man.'

Sartorial inelegance? Not pukka sahib behaviour, so Dennis was excluded from the team. No concession seems to have been made by Jammy James towards a lad already a year old for his form and who seemed to have done his best to put the previous year behind him. Loss of self-esteem could be damaging for a thirteen year old.

Dennis went into the second form, but as the year moved on, boredom again took over. He once more decided that he could find more interests elsewhere. We have already seen how Dennis' chance meeting with a US army officer had kindled an enthusiasm for maps. Yet what did he do when he played truant?

'If I skipped school, I could choose, for myself, where and how I spent my day. My driving passion at all times was travel. Where to, how to get there, what was there on arrival. In inclement weather I would visit the main line train stations. The bustle, the noise, the people, the trains. Where were they going? What were they doing? What was at the end of their journey?

The museums, libraries and the Regents Park Zoo had answers to many of these questions, and created even more. I would sit in libraries and read encyclopaedias and Bradshaw railway guides. These were of much greater interest than a regimented classroom. News theatres were small cinemas showing an hour or so of short films. They had newsreels, travelogues, short interest films etc. I acquired a wealth of knowledge ... It was not that I did not like the Grammar, it was that I could spend so much time there and not discover the things in which I had an interest.

Another learning experience that I had was at the local Ritz cinema. I had been befriended by the 'General Factotum' who tended the boilers, doubled as Commissionaire, supervised the cleaners and cared for the security during performances. In exchange for assisting him in some of these, I was allowed in the projection box. I learned about film making, distribution and exhibition. I learned about the power and operation of arc lights. I was also able to see films and newsreels of the day. It was here that I first saw the invasion of Europe, the subsequent battles and the atrocities of the concentration camps.'

No safety nets were erected in those days by the School to catch someone whose position at the School was becoming untenable. In 1947, Dennis' career at Hampton did come to an end, in a manner that was both salutary and painful and may have done his Headmaster little credit.

'Once more Mother and I were invited to an evening meeting with Mr Mason. It was decided that I was to be punished for constant truancy, but no mention was made as to what the punishment would be. I was to be allowed to end my time at Grammar at term's end. This being settled, I duly reported for school the following day. During the morning I was called from class to go to the Head's study where I received six of the best.

Having finished my time at Grammar, I was faced with finding employment. I applied to the GPO but failed the medical. I found temporary employment at a nearby factory.'

'A Grammar School Failure?' This question was answered when Dennis Barnes retired fifty years later, full of honours, from a distinguished career in public service in Australia.

War's End

The war in Europe ended on 8 May, 1945. Some believe, perhaps in retrospect, that the end had been eleven months coming, that the successes of D-Day, on land, at sea and in the air, made an Allied victory inevitable. However, the doodlebugs and V2s and the Nazi counter-offensive in the Ardennes in December 1944 shook any complacency that may have existed. Despite the invasions of Germany from the east and the west and the diplomatic unity shown by the Big Three, even President Roosevelt, speaking in front of the newsreel cameras at the Yalta Conference in February 1945, warned, *'The wars – and I mean wars – are not over yet.'*

For Mike Tadman, the end of the blackout, on 24 April, seemed to have been a signal that the end of the war was only a matter of time:

'That first evening I took a bus to Twickenham ... and I shall never forget the magic of it all. The street lamps were all on, every house was ablaze, and the cars and buses all had their headlamps unmasked. After five years of total darkness it was like fairyland.'

Compared with a world that had turned upside down on the Hanworth Road in September 1939, the end of the war in Europe had much less of an immediate effect on the School. Michael Savage remembers the impact at school as *'unremarkable'*, little more than *'a winding down'*. Robin Bligh recalls: *'We had known for several days that the fighting in Europe was ending, and in the evening of 7 May we heard that an armistice had been signed. The next day was VE Day and the 8th and 9th were a national holiday. Two or three weeks later I was taking School Certificate exams.'*

Away from school, on the two public holidays, it was different. Bob Smith remembers street parties at home in Feltham. Things got more out of hand in Hampton village where some wooden fences were torn down and used to build a large bonfire, crowned by an effigy of 'Adolf', a Verey Light in each hand and fireworks up his trousers. Jack Wells enjoyed the quieter festive parties on the Manor Estate nearby. People went up to London where there were vast scenes of riotous enjoyment. Mike Tadman and his mother went up on VE day. *'The whole city was in a state of delirium. In the middle of it all, Churchill drove down Whitehall, standing up in an open car. At one point I was walking alongside him, and was close enough to touch him had I wanted to.'*

It would be untrue to say that Victory in Europe was not celebrated at all at the School. Empire Day, on Thursday 24 May, provided the most appropriate occasion to commemorate the passing of war near to home, even though there were Commonwealth troops still engaged in desperate fighting with the Japanese in imperial spheres of influence in South-East Asia and the Pacific.

A special Empire Day programme was devised for the occasion at the School. About a third of the School turned up in uniform. In addition to 110 members of the Grammar School's ATC and Scout troop, units and troops from ATCs, Boy Scouts and Sea Scouts attended from elsewhere in Middlesex. First, a service was held in the hall. It was, of course, heavily patriotic, with hymns by Elgar, Holst and Parry, including 'England', and poetry by Newbolt and Rupert Brooke. The address was delivered not by the Headmaster, but by Flight Lieutenant Harry Crocker, who for so long had been the leading light in the ATC. The Lion's correspondent, *'RJB'* [Ray Blackwood] reported that Crocker *'... spoke of the Empire which meant so much to Britain, of the songs which had been written about it and of what the Empire had done for Britain in both in war and peace.'*

The assembled company then moved out to the front of the school:

'At 10.10, the Army Cadets and other units came to attention, Mr Crocker brought the School to attention and Troop-Leader JA Fewster broke the Union Jack on the flag-staff on the Tower. As it fluttered in the light breeze, Mr SJ House called for "Three Cheers for the Old Flag", and the cheers echoed in the morning air, a fitting end to a ceremony that will be remembered by Hamptonians as the first Victory Empire Day.'

The Pacific War ended quite suddenly during the summer holidays, after the dropping of atomic bombs on Japanese homeland targets. So there were no celebrations at School, and VJ Day, on Tuesday 15 August, was an anti-climax for civilians after the ecstatic celebrations in May. VJ Day was more important to those in the armed forces, not least the miraculous disappearance of the very real prospect of being shipped off to the Far East to engage in more bloody fighting. At last, the men and women service folk would be coming home, but it would be to Austerity Britain, where most of the rationing and other restrictions would continue for some years.

That is not to say the summer and the day did not have its memories for young Hamptonians. For 127 out of a record entry of 140 Hamptonians for the public examination that summer it was indeed a time to celebrate. All passed either their GSC or Highers examinations. 15 August 1945 found Bob Smith up in Wales with a couple of pals, in a tent overnight on a Rhondda Valley mountain, which conferred a spectacular view of a lit up valley. Jack Wells' family had their first proper holiday of the war in August 1945 when they went down to Paignton. He recorded in his diary that on VJ Day the family went for a swim and then in the evening attended a concert party in a huge marquee. The highlight was a splendid performance by a Royal Canadian Air Force band. Then, Wells says, *'... came a very amateur dramatic performance by the Paignton Players. My mother had to stuff a handkerchief in her mouth to stop herself hooting at the most solemn part of the proceedings. Finally, a great bonfire was lit to celebrate the day.'*

For 15 year old John Lovesey, after his brush with a flying bomb almost a year previous to the day, VJ Day was especially poignant:

'I went up to London with my uncle to see what was happening ... We wandered into Westminster Abbey and there was a service of celebration for the end of the war. We had just walked into the Abbey and sat down. Churchill, Attlee, Greenwood, all the ministers, Tedder – they were all there. We were part of that celebration!'

Summer 1945
(Ron Keevil)

Alfred Sidell Mason

An abiding memory of former Hampton Grammar School pupils during the war is that of their dark-clad, homburg-hatted Headmaster, Alfred Mason, *'stately and upright on an old-fashioned "sit-up-and beg" bicycle'*, pedalling up Nightingale Road to the School. To them he was iron-clad, invulnerable: if the Turk had failed to kill him at Kut, the Luftwaffe was sure to fail. Only one living being had the temerity to challenge this magisterial bicyclist. There dwelt a small white terrier half way up Nightingale Road. It loved passers-by, especially those on bicycles. When Bossy rode by, it chased him relentlessly, spurred on by the cheers of the likes of Jack Wells and his friends. Such, though, is the stuff of legend. 'Cheered on'? Surely not, surely sotto voce. No-one mocked the Headmaster; not even the formidable 'ole Jago' dared take his name in vain. According to John Lovesey, one unfortunate first former, Fred Potter, came late for Jago's french lesson, in only his second week at the School:

"'Potter! Where have you been?"

"I've been to see Mr Mason, sir."

"Mr Mason? Mr Mason!? Does anyone in this form know a Mr Mason?"

Some of us put up our hands and said: "Please, sir, he's the Headmaster."

Jago, his voice rising: "The Headmaster. You called the Headmaster Mr Mason!? I don't call him that! You call him The Headmaster!!"'

It would be repetitious to summarise all that has gone before in this account in respect of the Headmaster's command of his school, through what has been

The Headmaster
(David Franklin)

described as commitment, discipline, service and self-sacrifice. Emergency organisation, PWD, Blitz procedures, the dining commissariat, the School's diverse and effective war-effort had been led and held together by the prodigious efforts of Alfred Mason and his staff. Sometimes he had almost to admit defeat. Mason was a stickler for detail. The School List had to be right, the names of each boy recorded exactly. However, his records were only as good as the information given him. Was he told of David Fraenkel's change of surname by deed poll? There were double-barrelled surnames about which he had known nothing for years. And then there was the chaos of war: it must have been tiresome not quite knowing, at times, who was coming, who was present, who was going, who had gone, or who was returning. As for the mistresses' titles of address, the Headmaster admitted in a Governors' Meeting in 1946 that this had vexed him beyond measure.

For one small boy, though, a Mason administrative quirk had an unexpected legacy. Vic Rice-Smith remembers:

'I had to attend the Headmaster as Form Captain on one occasion and I was the first outside his door. He appeared from inside and said he would be back shortly, so go in and tell the others to follow suit. When I entered I was horrified to see many letters and papers over the floor underneath the window which was open. Being a considerate boy, I carefully picked them all up and put them on an adjacent table. When Bossy Mason returned he was shocked and horrified at my tidiness and was nearly apoplectic as he explained that this was his work system! He spread his work out in its priority for action – in effect this was his pending tray! Naturally, I felt about 2'6" tall! I have used, and still do use this system, and it works ...!'

Many years after his retirement Mason had his detractors, some of whom thought him insufficiently ambitious for his senior pupils. Against this it has to be said that he operated under significant constraints. The financial consequences of the Depression and the war had taken its toll of 16 year olds easily clever enough to go to university. The County Authority Awards – otherwise known as Scholarships – lasted for five, not seven years. So only a small minority stayed on in the sixth form to take Higher School Certificate, essential for university entrance. Free state-school education did not arrive till 1945, and within five years Mason had retired. Yet, he had already begun to reverse the trend: more Hamptonians were staying on in the sixth form and winning greater numbers of university and specialist places at institutions of higher learning in the sciences and technology. More were finding their way to Oxbridge – a record twelve undergraduate Old Hamptonians were in residence in 1950. The School was already enjoying the legacy of a Redbrick and Cambridge man perennially and – it has to be said – ruthlessly devoted to good public examination results.

Mason also seems to have been aware of barriers to social mobility for even the brightest from a modest background. This may be why he chipped away at the 'local accent', through the spoken word in school public speaking competitions and even in School Assembly. Dennis Barnes recalls:

'The bane of 'Bossy's' life was the hymn that started, "Holy, Holy, Holy." Shortly after a rousing start of "Howly, Howly, Howly," he would call "Stop! Stop! Stop! I will not have this Middlesex accent at this school." So, the opening line was repeated again and again until he was satisfied.'

Mason's rule was personal: he always made it his business to know all his boys. While less than sympathetic towards academic failures, he may have made up for this in his genuine concern, as we have seen, for those in difficulty caused by 'That Man'. And, even in retirement Bossy never forgot. Mike Tadman is still astonished:

'Twenty years after I left, I sent him a Christmas card, signed "Michael, Joyce and John Tadman". He wrote to me, saying "I assume that the other two people on your card are Joyce, your wife, and John, your son, named after your brother" ... During my time at the School, we only knew each other by our surnames, and I left the School in my third year ...'

Postscript

Just how lucky the School had been in the face of enemy action since 1939, on the one hand, and yet, on the other, with what optimism the School could face the future, were the two main thrusts of the Headmaster's first post-war report to the Governors, on 9 October 1945.

'At the end of the six years of war, during which much injury and much damage has been suffered locally, we connected with this School have cause to be very grateful for our own good fortune. One boy was killed in his own home in November 1940; one was crushed by a collapsed house about three years later but recovered completely in a few months.[44] Mr Yarrow's home was completely destroyed in August 1944 and many of the staff and boys have suffered damage to their homes of course. In this building

---

44   This pupil's identity is not known

two panes of glass were broken and one door fastening was burst open ... Among Old Boys the loss is very different, of course, about a hundred having died ...

The School was built to accommodate 650. There are 676 on the registers this term. Two unusual features are worth noting. One is that the middle school forms are practically full, evidence that very few boys are leaving at fourteen and fifteen. The other is the excessive size of the Science Sixth, which is now 48 strong. This number is far too large and I should like to break the form into two. That means of course getting an additional master.

All evacuees are now back.'

The Headmaster also reflected on the wartime public examination results, views that have been discussed elsewhere in this account. It is clear, though, that the results of the summer of 1945 compared favourably with those of the summer 1939, which the Headmaster as having described as *'excellent'*.

Behind this justified display of optimism, however, the dawn of peace-time brought a shepherd's warning for the Headmaster and the Governors, as they were already well aware. The 1944 Education Act had heralded a wind of change in education. From March 1945, Governors' meeting minutes reveal an increasing concern for the future status of the School. Two initiatives were recorded at the March meeting. First, in reaction to the Act which would abolish all fees in maintained schools, the Governors affirmed that *'Hampton Grammar School is a voluntary school under the provisions of the Act and the Governors wanted it to remain so'*. Second, while the principle of free state-education was not at issue, the future of an independently constituted Governing Body was. Under the Act, the position of the Governors was uncertain. It was recorded that the Governors had raised with the Ministry of Education the stipulations of the 1910 scheme, under which the Governors would hold office till the appointment of their successors. The Governors had requested information as to whether at 31 March 1945, *'... the Governors would continue to function and account for what business they may transact'*. It is no wonder that the Governors and the Headmaster were concerned about the School's measure of independence, for among other 'good works' they performed was their annual deployment of the Endowment Fund for bursaries to leaving Hamptonians destined for higher education, and in particular *'teacher training, dentistry, engineering, agriculture and training as a naval officer'*.

The position of the Governors had still not been resolved by 18 June 1945 when they next met. Therefore, at that meeting the Headmaster sought and received the Governors' support in taking *'necessary action for the running of the School'*. From September 1945, state school fees were a thing of the past, yet already there were strong hints of political battles ahead that would threaten Hampton as a grammar school, a story that lies beyond the scope of this book, but which is recorded in 'School by the Thames'.

The Governors had a good war. In a sense, their finest hour was even before September 1939, in the creation of the new school and facilitating the move after July, even though this was far from complete by September. For the next six years, beyond the confines of their termly meetings, an occasional special convention to discuss, for instance, a pupil disciplinary matter, and their prominence on Speech Days, the Governors worked very much in the background. Not recorded in the minutes of Governors' meetings before or during the war, for instance, were the deliberations of the Finance Committee, even though the general expenditure on staff salaries and Foundation awards to Old Hamptonians bound for university, amongst other items, were logged in that record.[45] As was the custom, they left the running of the School to the Headmaster.

One matter, though, that the Governors must have debated at length in their earlier meetings in 1943 was the future of Saturday morning school. In February, the Headmaster set out the arguments for and against its retention, instancing a rare consultation of the staff on a key matter. What was Mason's personal view? This was not recorded. His work ethic might suggest he would have favoured retention. Memories of boys playing in Carlisle Park instead of studying on 'free' mornings during the Blitz may have prompted one of his arguments in favour of retention. That having been said, the Governors moved with the times, and the Headmaster must have concurred. Moreover, his record would suggest that it would have been out of character for him to take a stand on such an issue, given the prevailing views and circumstances. More free time for staff and pupils, the exigencies of war as well as the County Authority's views against Saturday classes were cited in the Governors' decision, in May 1943, in favour of abolition, with the proviso that the matter might be re-visited at the end of the war. It never was, and the decision proved to be the most enduring on any policy matter taken by the Governors during the Second World War.

It was thus of paramount importance that there was mutual support between Governors and Headmaster on every issue. Although the Governors' hand may largely have been invisible, although the partnership may not have got it all right as in the case of academic policy and there was trouble ahead in the wake of the 1944 Education Act, there is no hint of disruption to the oneness between Governors and Headmaster.

---

45 On principle, pupil fee books and the minutes of the Finance Committee have not been used in the author's research, given the sensitive nature of specific fee details of pupils.

Gradually, normal service was resumed at the School. On top of the excellent public examination results in the summer of 1945, the autumn term produced one of the School's best Oxbridge entries. Some of the masters returned, Gassy Garside having spent his last few months in uniform writing his war memoirs. One by one the Lady *'Sirs'* left, the revered Miss GR Harrison the last to leave in 1946. It took more than a year to get the ditches filled in and longer for the fields to recover, but young Hamptonians were soon playing all the sport they wanted. The concrete air-raid shelters lasted into the reign of Gavin Alexander.

Of the extra-mural school activities spawned by war, the two most remarkable were the ATC and the Pig Club. The ATC's popularity was scarcely diminished, its commanding officer awarded a deserved MBE. Sixty-three years later the unit continues to thrive as part of the School's Combined Cadet Force. The Pig Club too had its devotees at the end of the war, but it would last only as long as its white Yorkshire sow. Even though The Lion of the autumn 1945 paid tribute to the sow's fecundity – it had produced at least two litters – the magazine announced the imminence of the sow's departure for the bacon production line. Neither a long service medal nor a replacement were forthcoming. By 1947 the area behind the bicycle sheds had been turned over to the Young Farmers' Club, which in due course was also to become a casualty of post-war necessity.

What has been far harder to reflect, let alone quantify, in this account, is the degree of anguish inflicted by war, directly or indirectly, on members of the School or their families. It was one thing to be irritated by the move from the cosy familiarity of the Old School to the shiny modernity of the Hanworth Road emporium, another to endure the sudden terror of being buried alive in one's home. The eye-witnesses do not always recall their feelings in the worst of times. As a survivor of the Mesopotamian campaign in the Great War, Bossy Mason may have been as hardened as any to the emotions of war. Yet Hampton Grammar School was 'his regiment'. Scarcely a fortnight would pass after 1939 than he would have to announce in Assembly to 'the regiment', the death of yet another of 'his' Old Boys on active service, and the final total of Old Hamptonian dead was 122.[46] In February 1945, Mason's predecessor, WA Roberts, another great headmaster of the Grammar and also known as 'Bossy', passed on. Even after the end, in October 1945 – when the dying was supposed to have stopped – one of the most difficult announcements for the Headmaster to make must have been of the death of a third successive Captain of School, Dick Rudkin, while on a peace-time training flight in Germany. 'Must have been' difficult? A guess? Bossy

---

46   The 1939-1945 War Memorial is situated between the foyer and the hall at Hampton School

has left sufficient clues for us to gauge the depth of his compassion, in the wartime Lion's 'Notes from the Headmaster's Desk', a voluminous and personal record of his contact with more than five hundred serving Old Boys and Staff; and in his description of Bill Yarrow's reaction to the news of the destruction of his home in Sunbury in August 1944.

Coping with such Assemblies would have been difficult for most present. So many never forgot. Ken Skelton has reflected on the effect that Bert Cheeseman's death had on him. Stan Tanner provides a rare insight, talking of his own unspoken feelings when bad news broke:

'I do not know how other fellows felt but Kenny Porter and I who were confidants in most things, never discussed any thoughts of danger. Certainly we listened to daily news of our troops across the world and felt for them, especially those from Hampton. The growing list of OH men killed in action, read out at morning prayers left us bereft and silent.

Early in 1944, as an offensive seemed increasingly likely, we were talking to our form master [EM Harrison] and he told us that his son had come back from army training in Canada – 'just in time for this do,' he said, nodding towards the Channel. A few months later he was killed in Normandy. It was about this time, too, that my friend from junior school showed us a telegram that his mother had received, saying that his elder brother had been killed in the Air Force ...

That is why I said a prayer when we knew that in Europe, at least, it was all over'.

Old Yellow Face kept perfect time 1939-1945

Form 5B - Hampton Grammar School - Summer Term 1946.

(John Lovesey)

18 JA Tanner   19 AW Goffe   20 GA Beechey   21 BL Terry   22 JG Sporton   23 MH Cope   24 Mr C Mulley   25 JG Turner   26 BF Bransden   27 PA Glenister   28 RH Hart

8 SP Scott   9 WJE Barlow   10 RHN Prydderch   11 RE Head   12 CW Goodridge   13 FJP Syrad   14 JM Williams   15 JR Lovesey   16 AE Cook   17 AP Bigg

1 DG Philips   2 IM Willis   3 JM Mercer   4 RW Brett   5 PA Heims   6 MT Simpson   7 AD Baldry

IN PROUD AND AFFECTIONATE MEMORY OF THE FOLLOWING
OLD HAMPTONIANS WHO GAVE THEIR LIVES IN THE WAR OF 1939-45

J. BANKS D.F.C	D. W. EVES	R. G. JAMES	V. MURRAY	L. E. STOCKWELL
D. V. BARKER	R. H. FOKES D.E.C. D.F.M.	C. E. JOHNSON	D. R. MUSSELLWHITE	M. A. STRATTON
E. A. BENJAMIN D.F.C.& Bar	E. M. FORD	N. H. JOHNSON	R. J. NAPIER (A.L.A)	R. L. STREATHER
E. H. D. BEYER	R. L. GIBSON	P. KINCAID	J. B. P. NORMAN	D. I. P. STURT
K. V. BOTT	R. E. GILBERT	D. G. KING	F. J. OTTERWAY	I. F. THOMAS
J. S. BRITTER	E. G. GITTINGS	W. A. KING	S. OWEN	W. H. THOMLINSON
F. J. BROAD	D. E. GLOYNS	J. B. KNIGHT	B. G. PACKER	W. D. TIGHE
K. A. BROAD	L. A. GREEN	G. LAUDER	R. G. PAPWORTH	J. H. TOLKIEN
H. W. BUTT	P. L. GREEN	G. C. H. LAUENER	B. A. W. PENN	R. R. TURNER
G. W. D. CARTER	N. O. GURNEY	A. P. LINSDELL	J. J. PERRY	R. V. (WARREN) WALKER
D. J. S. CHAPMAN	J. S. HARMAN	A. E. LIVERSIDGE	W. K. B. PHILLIPSON	D. J. WALMSLEY
B. CHEESEMAN	J. H. HARRIS	P. J. LONGWORTH	F. J. PILE D.F.C.	H. F. WATSON
R. R. L. CLARK	L. R. HAWLEY	J. W. MACDOUGALL	R. C. PLATT	D. N. WENHAM
I. T. CLEMENT M.C.	A. McP. HAY	R. A. L. MARLEY	L. P. PLUM	C. S. K. WHALEY
K. G. W. CLIFTON	A. W. HAY	J. W. MARSTON	W. H. POOLE	C. A. WHITE
N. P. COLLINS	W. D. HEAP	K. J. MEARS	A. H. RADBOURNE	G. J. WHITE
C. H. CORNISH	E. J. H. HEATHER	R. L. MEATYARD	R. C. RUDKIN	R. H. WILKINSON
H. DAWES	E. W. HEATHER	C. G. MILES	R. E. RUSSELL	C. WILSON
I. F. DELL	L. R. HEBBERD	L. N. MILLIS	A. H. SEVERN	D. J. WOOD
A. E. DIBLEY	A. E. HIGGINS	H. A. H. MILLS	J. SIMPSON	F. C. WOOD
J. A. DRAPER	J. A. HOBBS	J. C. MILLS	G. D. SINGLETON	R. C. WOOD
E. G. R. DROBIG	A. E. HORWELL	R. P. MOLLETT	H. J. SPIERS	F. G. WOODS
A. F. EASTMAN	B. H. H. JAMES	F. W. P. MOTT	D. W. STANTIALL	E. E. G. YOUSEMAN D.F.C.
D. L. EDWARDS				

P. KENNARD   J. J. WATSON

Bibliography

Primary sources

diaries:
David Franklin
Pat Gubbins
Peter Hornsby, extracts from The Lion, 1989

Hampton School Archives:
Minutes of Governors' Meetings, 1939-1945
School lists, prospectus, 1939-1945
School Rules and Customs, 1935; 1942
The Lion, 1939-2007
Old Hamptonian Chronicle, 1946-2007
Mason, AS: Russia account - "Hampton Grammar School": description of Hampton Grammar School, commissioned by UK Ministry of Education for USSR Commissariat for Education, June 1945

newspapers:
Richmond and Twickenham Times
Middlesex Chronicle

photographs:
English Heritage; David Franklin; Getty Images; Hampton School Archives; Imperial War Museum; Ron Keevil; Betty Knight; Lincolnshire County Archives; John Lovesey; Alan Meacock; and John Sheaf

publicity pamphlet covers:
HM Government, published in wartime (HMSO, now TSO)

London Borough of Richmond upon Thames, Local Studies Collection:
Records of the Blitz, Borough of Twickenham
Register of Incidents
Register of Air Raid casualties admitted to hospital
Map of Bomb Incidents

telegram: from Imperial Scouting HQ to *Ian Cameron*

eye-witness reminiscences, written submissions:
Barnes, Dennis, OH (1943-1947): e-mail, 2007
Bligh, Robin, OH (1940-1947): e-mail, letter, 2008
Blackwood, Ray, OH (1940-1946): e-mail, 2008
Cleall, Charles, OH (1942-1944): e-mail, 2008
Fisher, Derek, OH (1943-48), and his brother David: e-mail, 2007
Holtom, Stan, OH (1942-1948): e-mail, letter, 2008
Meacock, Alan, OH (1936-1942): letter, 2007
Rice-Smith, Vic, OH (1944-1950): letter, 2008
Smith, RW 'Bob', OH (1944 -1949): letter, 2008
Tadman, Mike, OH (1940-1943): letter, 2007
Tanner, Dr Stan, OH (1937-1943): e-mail, letter, 2007 and 2008
Warmington, John, OH (1941-1947): letter, 2007

Oral submissions and conversations, tape-recorded or noted:

Duddy, Alan, OH (1939-1944): recorded interview, 2008
Gubbins, Pat, OH (1936 -1940): noted conversations, and his written accompanying notes, 2008
Lovesey, John, OH (1940-1946): recorded interview, 2007
Mabb, Clive, OH (1942-1949): noted conversations, 2008
Meacock, Alan, OH (1936-1942): telephone conversation, 2008
Rippengal, Derek, CB OH (1939-1947): noted conversation
Savage, Michael, OH (1943-1949): recorded interview, 2008
Skelton, Ken, OH (1939-1943): recorded interview, 2007
Warmington, John, OH (1941-1947): noted telephone conversation, 2008
Wells, Jack, OH (1939 -1946): recorded interview, 2007

Reminiscences, printed:

Brown, Marjory, (HM's secretary, 1933-1948): article in OH Chronicle, Sept 1990
Cusworth, David, OH (1938-1943): letter to Ken Rice, reprinted in The Lion, 1994
Hodges, Peter, OH (1939-1944): in OH Chronicle 2007
Jago, HWT, staff: retirement interview in The Lion, summer 1963
Kerpner, George, OH (1939-45): in OH Chronicle, 2007
Lovesey, John, OH (1940-46): in OH Chronicle 2007
Mabb, Clive, OH (1942 – 1949): in OH Chronicle 2006
Mason, AS, OBE: article in The Lion, spring 1953
Mills, Peter, OH (1939-1943): in OH Chronicle, October 2002
Styan, Joan: in BBC WW2 People's War – Archive List 2756298
Tanner, Dr Stan, OH (1936-1943): reminiscences, in OH Chronicle 2007

Autobiography:

Brudenell, Michael, OH (1937-1944): 'My Life – the first 80 years, 1925 - 2005', (private publication 2007)
Catford, Sir Robin, KCVO OH (1935-1941): draft private memoir (not published)
Claxton, John, OH (1940-1945): 'Ginger's Back', privately published on web
Franklin, David, OH (1938-1943): 'Dave's Tales', Guild Press, 2008

Secondary sources

Barnfield, Paul: 'When the Bombs Fell: Twickenham, Teddington and the Hamptons under Aerial Bombardment during the Second World War', Borough of Twickenham Local History Society, 2001
Chorley, WR: 'RAF Bomber Command Losses of the Second World War', Ian Allan
Garside, Bernard: 'A Brief History of Hampton School 1557-1957', private publication, 1957
James, WD: 'Hamptonians at War', private publication. Final chapter on the School during the war, by *AS Mason*
Longmate, Norman: 'How We Lived Then: A History of Everyday Life during the Second World War', published by Hutchinson. Reprinted by permission of The Random House Group Ltd.
Rice, K A (ed): 'Garside's Wars', Hampton School, 1993. Part Two
Wild, Edward and *Rice, Ken:* 'School by the Thames: The Story of Hampton School', James and James, 2005

INDEX OF NAMES
(Names beneath appear in main text and photographs)